CABARET PERFORMANCE

Volume I: Europe 1890-1920

*This book is dedicated to the memory of Jacques Chwat,
who was the most European of Americans*

Library of Congress Cataloging in Publication Data
Cabaret Performance: Volume I. Europe 1890-1920
Library of Congress Catalog Card No.: 88-62672
ISBN: 1-55554-042-2 (cloth)
ISBN: 1-55554-043-0 (paper)

Printed in the United States of America

Publication of this book has been made possible in part by grants received from the National Endowment for the Arts, Washington, D.C., a federal agency, and the New York State Council on the Arts.

This translation has been made possible in part through a grant from the Wheatland Foundation, New York.

CABARET PERFORMANCE

Volume I: Europe 1890-1920

Sketches, Songs, Monologues, Memoirs

selected and translated, with commentary, by

Laurence Senelick

PAJ Publications
New York

4

CONTENTS

FOREWORD

GRANDIOSITY WAS THE KEYNOTE OF THE NINETEENTH CENTURY. In politics, it was manifested in an encroaching imperialism, a hardening nationalism, a swelling militarism. In commerce, industrialization centered in vast factory complexes and widespread monopolies. In the arts, grandiosity took shape as the three-volume novel, as the five-act sensational melodrama with elaborate scenic effects, as the huge academic genre painting with its hundreds of significant details, as massive expositions, grand opera and, of course, Wagner's *Gesamtkunstwerk*.

By the end of the century, reaction had set in against this gigantism. The Arts and Crafts movement sought to return the artisanal process to its individual human contributors. Aesthetic poets repudiated the epic in favor of limited lyric forms like the villanelle and triolet. And in the performing arts, the significantly named little théâtre movement, exemplified by the Théâtre Libre in Paris and the Intima Teatern in Stockholm, eschewed commercial compromise by staging subtly performed one-acts or chamber productions of an experimental nature.

The one-act, whether offered as a "slice-of-life" by the naturalists or as a study in mood by the symbolists, exemplifies this deliberate rejection of the grandiose. It condensed the artistic experience into a quintessence meant to have an immediate impact on the spectator. The performance cabaret was an offshoot of this reaction. Although it bore different names and natures at different times in the course of its development, the cabaret essentially defined the genre the Germans call *Kleinkunst* and the Russians "theatre of miniatures": art that is minor not in significance or intentions but reduced in scale to its essential components. It partook of the aesthetic atmosphere of its time to no small degree. It is no coincidence that many of the best songs of the artistic cabaret were intentionally naturalistic in language, theme, or local color, while certain of its devices, such as the shadow-play, were both decadent and symbolist in their use of light, color, and evocative suggestion. The cabaret playlet was a miniaturization of the already compact one-act, and would gradually dwindle into the "blackout" sketch of the postwar revue, a cartoon with a punchline caption.

Cabaret was also inspired, to a large extent, by variety which, over the course of the nineteenth century, had evolved as a highly commercialized species of urban popular entertainment. By 1890, variety theatres had themselves become grandiose, elaborate palaces of stereotyped amusement. But the innovators of the cabaret intended to distil from the vaudeville, circus, and music halls their vitality, immediacy, and vivacity; to adopt the rapid alternation of attractions; and then, to harness these demotic features in order to convey a rarefied artistic style or a liberal political message or a skewed vision of the world. What proved attractive to the early cabaretists and their coteries was the play element, the sense that art did not have to be uplifting or earnest. Most serious artists had despaired of the boulevard theatre, because its commercially viable forms, the farce and the melodrama, struck them as beneath contempt; yet the artistically serious theatre, the pilgrimages to Bayreuth and the darkened auditoriums for versitic stagings of Ibsen, Hauptmann, and problem drama, seemed to many to be fatally dismal, crepe-draped mirrors of the middle-class sensibility. The first propagandists for cabaret wanted the spectator to smoke, drink, comment, and join in the chorus as he would at a music hall; they wanted to reclaim the theatre for sensuality and mirth. The components of pop art were to be the medium of high art. And in the process, a new audience would be won for the avant-garde. As the dramatist Frank Wedekind saw it, the cabaret was to serve as "a most valuable intermediate stage between the impoverishment of the cultural proletariat and what is acknowledged to be literature."

In his book *Munich and Theatrical Modernism*, Peter Jelavich has coined the term "cabaretic modernism" to label this phenomenon. Many of the most exciting innovations in twentieth-century performance art began in cabarets. Emerging from bohemian haunts, the cabaret was the earliest podium for the expressionists, the DADAists, the futurists; it was a congenial forum for experiments in shadowgraphy, puppetry, free-form skits, jazz rhythms, literary parody, "naturalistic" songs, "bruitistic" litanies, agitprop, dance-pantomime, and political satire. As it sublimated and converted variety entertainment, it in turn ramified and affected revues, night clubs, *tours de chant*, and other less exclusive amusements.

To adopt a characteristic cited by Petra-Maria Einsporn, the cabaret's stance was essentially "antinomian": it took up an adversarial position towards accepted moral attitudes and assailed them by means of satire. Pre-war cabarets were not, however, as politically engaged as the cabarets of the 20s and 30s would be. Censorship in the German, Russian, and Austro-Hungarian empires prevented outspoken treatment of current abuses in domestic and foreign policy. In France and Italy, political commitment was often vitiated by a *je-m'en-foutiste* (*who gives a damn?*) attitude. Rather, the policies of most literary and artistic cabarets were essentially but generally anti-establishment, directing their shafts at such pillars of society as bourgeois prejudices and values, conventional morality, academic art, and capitalist economy. From the Hydropathes to the DADA and futurist movements, the form cut a wide swath of anarchy, dismissing reform or reconstruction in favor of the demolition of existing institutions: the resulting chaos was supposed to promote fresh artistic creativity. In this respect, the Great War was seen as a liberating force, the logical culmination of the inequities and idiocies of society, and in its wake, cabarets would enjoy wider popular appeal but, paradoxically, less audacity in experimentation. (See *Cabaret Performance: Europe 1920-1940*)

The cabaret was primarily a European form, sprung from small, discrete groups of artists and playing, at least at the start, to a relatively homogenous audience. Those who envisage cabaret as the sort of club Sally Bowles performs in in the homonymous musical should be forewarned: that was the kind of "amusement cabaret" most pre-war artists looked down on (although it later gained a kind of artistic cachet when run by exceptional creators) and its mixed audience of tourists, profiteers, drag queens, and Brown Shirts is far more miscellaneous than the real thing could have tolerated. In England and America, cabaret was taken to mean a night-spot with a certain amount of mindless diversion accompanying food and drink; popular entertainment was never threatened by its competition, particularly in Prohibition New York, where pleasure-seekers habituated Harlem jazz clubs and smart Greenwich Village revues, with no golden mean between these polarities.

But throughout Europe, cafés, restaurants, wine-cellars, derelict playhouses were converted into platforms for avant-garde drama, song, dance, comedy, prose. The degree of radicalism or sophistication would be determined by local conditions and individual talents, but in most cases the fundamental aim was the same—to provide a refined alternative to the entertainment establishment. Invariably, the more potent the performance, the shorter-lived it was. Before the first World War, economics often forced the artistic cabaret to open its doors to a wider public or go under; this meant that the core of advanced artists who had founded it would either be overwhelmed by the broader tastes of this less exclusive audience or would adapt and dilute their work to suit it. The development of Berlin's Schall und Rauch is a typical case in point. Beginning as a resort for theatre people specializing in parody, it soon turned into a theatre for experimental stagings of classics and new plays; revived in larger premises and dominated by DADAists, it failed, despite all the novelty of its approach, to put bums on seats and ended as an ordinary beerhall that offered incidental entertainment.

In this respect, the artistic cabaret followed the path that the music hall had already taken. Tavern singsongs, where the consumer would contribute his air when requested, had gradually developed into ''night cellars,'' where the clientele was diverted by professional or semi-professional singers; it was but a short step from this to the clearcut distinction between spectator in his theatre seat and paid performer on stage. Similarly, the earliest cabarets presented material written and performed by members of a small coterie for fellow-members. The introduction first of guests and then of paying customers coarsened the ambience and, eventually, the technique of the cabaret; so that the cabaret's avowed original intention of refining the music hall was betrayed as it turned into a music hall itself.

(A similar phenomenon may be observed in post-modernist performance art as well. As he is touted by the media and introduced to a wider public, the artist is hard-pressed to retain those jagged or subtle elements which characterize his style and brought him to the fore at the outset of his career. Comedians lobbing nuances at café tables, gay and lesbian performers playing to their brothers and sisters, miscalled "new vaudevillians" joking about Beckett to an audience of drama majors often seem anodyne and adrift when they strike it lucky and get co-opted by television, Broadway, and films.)

This anthology is meant as a sampler of types of cabaret performance throughout Europe from the inception of the *cabaret artistique* at the turn of the century to the upsurge of radical artistic experimentation during and after World War I. The emphasis is on the sketch rather than the song, since this genre has been relatively neglected by earlier works on cabaret, and because cabaret songs, in their topicality and ingenuity, require both their music and their original language to make an effective impression. When I have translated a song, however, I have attempted to preserve the original meter, imagery, and rhyme-scheme to the best of my ability. Certain cultures omitted in this volume, such as those of Austria, Czechoslovakia, Hungary, and Sweden, will be presented in the next, to be devoted to the cabaret from the end of the Great War to the Nazi ban on conférenciers in 1940.

This book owes a great deal to many persons who have offered counsel, encouragement, criticism, and assistance from the time I conceived it in a *Jugendstil* flat in West Berlin in 1985. These include, first of all, Berlin comrades who accompanied me on cabaret jaunts: Henry Akina, Christoff Bleidt, Alain Courtney, Dagmar Höher, Roy Kift, Joachim Klein, and Helen Palmer. Then there are those who provided expert linguistic advice: E. M. Beekman, Peter Jelavich, Tatyana Khaikin, Robert Konski, and Joshua Rifkin. Gesine Bottomley, Librarian, and her staff at the Bibliothek of the Wissenschaftskolleg zu Berlin, and the staff of the Harvard Theatre Collection helped locate obscure material. Joanne Barnett, Jon Crowder, and Sharon Mullen of the Tufts University Drama Department did epic amounts of photocopying. And finally, my editors Gautam Dasgupta and Bonnie Marranca, by their provocation and stimulation, made this collection broader and deeper than it might otherwise have been.

I

The Artistic Cabaret in France and Holland

1890-1917

IN THE BEGINNING WERE THE *HYDROPATHES*, FOUNDED IN PARIS IN 1878 by Emile Goudeau and four other young men. The name came, some say, from Goudeau's obsession with Gungl's *Hydropathen-Walz*; according to others, from the word's punning analogy with his own name: *Gout d'eau* = taste for water, *hydropathe* = water fancier. Eventually the group swelled to fifty congenial spirits, who met on Wednesdays and Saturdays between 9 and 12 p.m. for a little drinking and a lot of singing and recitation. They began to put out a journal the following year, the manifesto reading "Talent, whatsoever its origin, in whatsoever form it takes, will find a ready welcome here." The group's attitude was one of deadpan mockery (*fumisterie*), a poker-faced assault on all the totems of bourgeois life.

A leading light of the Hydropathes was Alphonse Allais (1854-1905), a fair-haired pharmacist from Honfleur, who enlivened the company with macabre shaggy-dog stories. He became a major contributor to the journal, his short pieces classics of punning and inconsequential black humor. When the Hydropathes organized their Incoherents' Salon, Allais exhibited his own music, with such pieces as "Funeral March Specially Composed for the Obsequies of a Deaf Dignitary," and his own paintings, such as an all-black canvas entitled "Negroes Fighting in a Cave by Night."

The Poor Slob and the Good Fairy is a prime example of the type of hydropathic humor that was to permeate the early artistic cabaret. Allais first published it as a story in *Le Chat Noir* in 1889, then rewrote it as a monologue delivered by Coquelin Cadet in 1891. It qualifies as a direct ancestor of what would become the standard cabaret sketch.

The Poor Slob and the Good Fairy

(Le Pauvre Bougre et le Bon Génie)

1899

by

Alphonse Allais

CHARACTERS:

The Poor Slob
The Waiter
The Good Fairy

(The outdoor seating at a modest café situated in an unfrequented street. Chairs, pedestal tables. The Waiter is wiping off the tables as he vocalizes, just like an opera singer exercising his voice; then he removes two empty glases.)

THE WAITER: La, la, la, la, la, la! Hem! Hem! Hem! Hem! Fantastic, I've never felt in such good voice as I do today. *(He sings.)*
 Oh, Matilda, idol of my soul!
What a voice! *(Bitterly.)* And I have to waste it serving stinking beers to a bunch of jerks who stiff you with a two-centime tip! . . . Curses! *(He sings.)*
 Undying glory of our forebears!
I could make a smash tonight at the suburban Grand Opera! . . . And if I say suburban, it's only because in my present state, I can't do myself justice! . . . And with this basso profundo too! . . . *(He gestures like a man who's making the best of things.)* Oh well! Now I'm starting to fret and fretting never got anybody

anywhere. So . . . (*He exits, singing.*)
What matter betrayals . . .

THE POOR SLOB: (*Enters, worn out, ever so worn out! and dressed in a suit that is clean but indescribably shapeless. He drops into a chair.*) Oh, sure, I've got my faults, and I don't pretend to be any more perfect than the next fellow, but one thing you can't deny is that I'm damned thirsty! I *am* thirsty! Throughout my long career, a career rich in all sorts of dry-spells, I don't think I've ever experienced the kind of thirst I've got now. (*He pulls a ten centime coin from his pocket and raps it on the table.*) Waiter! . . . Nothing gets you like walking up all those stairs, unless it's coming down them again. (*He raps again.*) Waiter! . . . If you put all the stairs I went up and down the last few weeks end to end, I bet I could climb to Olympus! (*He stops short.*) Wait, that scans! (*He declaims pompously.*)

I bet I could climb to Olympus!

It's not very elegant blank verse, but it's blank verse all the same. (*He raps more loudly on the table.*) Waiter! . . . If that waiter doesn't come soon, all he'll find in this seat will be a desiccated corpse.

THE WAITER: Coming, coming, on the wing!

THE POOR SLOB: And none too soon, if you don't mind my saying so.

THE WAITER: Ah! It's you, my poor monsieur! How are things going?

THE POOR SLOB: Ugh.

THE WAITER: Did you manage to find a job?

THE POOR SLOB: Not the slightest, alas! All the employers told me to try, try again some other time.

THE WAITER: (*Laughing stupidly.*) That must be very trying.

THE POOR SLOB: (*Shrugging.*) You think that's funny?

THE WAITER: Oh no! But you've got to laugh . . . So, an absinthe as usual?

THE POOR SLOB: No, no absinthe yet . . . I'm too thirsty. If you drink absinthe when you're thirsty, my friend, you blaspheme against your Creator! . . . Beer will meet my requirements.

THE WAITER: So, one glass of beer?

THE POOR SLOB: Just a plain glass of beer.

THE WAITER: Light? . . . Dark? . . .

THE POOR SLOB: Light! (*Abruptly changing his mind.*) No!

Dark.

THE WAITER: (*Exits, singing.*)
> The light one and the dark
> Play tennis with his heart.

THE POOR SLOB: He's singing the truth, the nitwit! My heart has never ceased to fluctuate between fair women and dark ones. There are some blondes who could have enticed me from all the brunettes in the world, but I've known some brunettes I would have given my life to possess . . . No offense meant to those young ladies with auburn hair and certain red-headed lassies.

THE WAITER: The beer you ordered!

THE POOR SLOB: (*Grabs the glass and empties it in one gulp, to the astonishment of the waiter.*) This beer isn't drinkable.

THE WAITER: (*Contemplating the empty glass.*) What would you have done if it were?

THE POOR SLOB: I would have asked for another one.

THE WAITER: (*Casually.*) Oh well, beer isn't our strong point here!

THE POOR SLOB: So I see.

THE WAITER: (*Changing the subject.*) So, back on the streets, my poor monsieur?

THE POOR SLOB: Forever, alas! . . . And my scanty savings are beginning to wear down. (*He counts his money.*) All I have to last out the year is one franc forty.

THE WAITER: That's pretty skimpy.

THE POOR SLOB: One franc forty! . . . This reserve capital which might seem sufficient to certain financial enterprises that shall remain nameless is rather slender for a single individual . . . Oh well! let us hope! and let us forget! Now, let me have an absinthe, my friend! Absinthe spells oblivion! Absinthe induces a blissful escape from this earthly prison we call life.

THE WAITER: (*Dreamily.*) Maybe so.

THE POOR SLOB: Sometimes you see a man in the gutter. You say, ''That man is drunk!'' No! He is running away.

THE WAITER: And the police march him off to the station house to teach him not to run away the next time . . . You want the absinthe neat?

THE POOR SLOB: No, with anisette.

THE WAITER: (*Exits singing to the tune of ''Alouette, Gentille Alouette.''*)
> Aniset-te, tasty aniset-te,

Aniset-te, I shall drink you down!

THE POOR SLOB: (*Alone.*) That man's high spirits are obscene! He makes me feel he has a job! And what a delightful occupation! A dispenser of oblivion! . . .

THE WAITER: (*Enters, singing.*)
'Tis absinthe
Makes the heart grow fonder.

THE POOR SLOB: Are you happy, my friend?

THE WAITER: Me? Not a chance, I am not happy!

THE POOR SLOB: But you are always singing.

THE WAITER: Just because a person sings doesn't mean he's happy.

THE POOR SLOB: Still . . .

THE WAITER: No, the fact is, I sing because I'm a singer.

THE POOR SLOB: A singer?

THE WAITER: Of course . . . I may look like an ordinary waiter, but I'm not! (*Drawing himself up.*) I am an opera singer.

THE POOR SLOB: Strange combination.

THE WAITER: Ah, my poor monsieur, it's a very sad story and . . . have you got a minute?

THE POOR SLOB: Have I got a minute! I've got a hundred, a thousand minutes! That's all I've got! Tell me your story, my friend.

THE WAITER: All right, and then you'll see you aren't the only hard-luck case in this world.

THE POOR SLOB: It's just that we aren't unionized.

THE WAITER: Picture this: a few years ago, I had made my debut as a waiter in a small restaurant near the Opéra-Comique . . . the old one, you know . . .

THE POOR SLOB: Yes, the one that burned down.

THE WAITER: Right . . . So, one fine day, some gentlemen, real gentlemen, journalists, discovered that I had a magnificent voice, that's the word, *magnificent*! Everyone predicted that I would get into the opera. I didn't waste a minute, I took singing lessons and a short time later, I made my debut at a small provincial theatre.

THE POOR SLOB: Congratulations!

THE WAITER: Yeah, sure! No sooner had I stepped on stage when I lost my voice. (*He points to his throat and imitates the behavior of a mute.*) No more voice than the palm of my hand! Ah! that was fun! . . . So I had to put my waiter's apron on again.

THE POOR SLOB: This profession is as good as any other.

THE WAITER: I don't agree . . . But let me finish. I had been serving beers and iced coffees for less than a week when my voice came back! . . . Thrilling, isn't it?

THE POOR SLOB: (*Coldly.*) Nothing thrills me.

THE WAITER: When I realized my voice had come back, what did I do? I took off my apron and got an engagement.

THE POOR SLOB: And then?

THE WAITER: (*Sadly.*) Oh, you can figure out the rest.

THE POOR SLOB: You lost your voice again?

THE WAITER: Exactly! And ever since then, it's always the same thing: a magnificent voice when I'm a waiter and zero when I have to sing *William Tell.*

THE POOR SLOB: The situation is not devoid of a certain piquancy. You know what you ought to do?

THE WAITER: Tell me.

THE POOR SLOB: Try to get a job in a music hall. You can sing your repertory while you serve the drinks.

THE WAITER: That's an idea. I'll think it over.

THE POOR SLOB: Alas! I don't have that resource. I am neither a singer nor a waiter. I am an accountant, an unemployed accountant, because my job was phased out.

THE WAITER: Don't give up hope, my poor monsieur, I'm sure you'll find a good job when you least expect it.

THE POOR SLOB: I'll accept your prediction, because my patience is at an end . . . All the walking, all the humiliation! . . .

THE WAITER: (*Gloomily.*) I know all about humiliation.

THE POOR SLOB: (*Philosophically.*) To tell you the truth, the humiliation's not so bad, my hide is now too callous to blush.

THE WAITER: (*Sarcastically.*) Your hat does your blushing for you.

THE POOR SLOB: (*Removing his hat and noting that it is, indeed, bright red.*) The fact is my topper's going rusty.

THE WAITER: On the other hand, your frockcoat's turning a pretty green.

THE POOR SLOB: Behold the mysteries of nature! Who can explain why Time, that strange colorist, enjoys turning our old hats red, while he paints ancient frockcoats green. (*He lays his hat alongside his coat-sleeve.*) The green of my coat contrasts admirably with the red of my headgear.

THE WAITER: And vice-versa.

THE POOR SLOB: Contrasted this way, my coat looks greener and my hat redder.

THE WAITER: It's not so ugly, when you think about it.

THE POOR SLOB: Nevertheless I would have preferred a less colorful outfit . . . When will I be able to treat myself to a new one from the department store?

THE WAITER: That's not much of an ambition.

THE POOR SLOB: I've never been ambitious. With five francs a day, I would be the happiest of mortals.

THE WAITER: Five francs a day! Not what I'd call striking it rich.

THE POOR SLOB: But I would be perfectly satisfied! Where is the good fairy who could guarantee me five francs a day?

(*Heavenly music is heard, abruptly interrupting their discussion.*)

THE GOOD FAIRY: A good fairy! Who speaks of a good fairy? . . . Here I am!

(*The Poor Slob and The Waiter fall into raptures and clasp their hands.*)

THE POOR SLOB: What! . . . You really are? . . .

THE GOOD FAIRY: A good fairy, yes . . . What's so surprising about that?

THE POOR SLOB: Oh nothing . . . I mean, it is! This sort of thing doesn't happen every day.

THE GOOD FAIRY: Were you the one who summoned me, poor slob?

THE POOR SLOB: I was.

THE GOOD FAIRY: You have done well, poor slob, for I am never invoked in vain. What can I do for you?

THE POOR SLOB: Just now I was telling this gentleman (*he indicates the Waiter*) that with five francs a day I would be the happiest of mortals.

THE GOOD FAIRY: (*Laughing.*) Five francs a day! Ah, poor slob, they can't accuse you of being greedy for gold.

THE POOR SLOB: That's just what I was saying to this gentleman. I've never been ambitious.

THE GOOD FAIRY: So, five francs a day will do it for you?

THE POOR SLOB: Amply.

THE GOOD FAIRY: Very well! Rejoice, poor slob. Your wish is about to be granted.

THE POOR SLOB: (*Jubilant.*) Really? You can do that for me?

THE GOOD FAIRY: Of course, you big booby, nothing to it . . . However, since I've got other things to do than bring you—what do you simple mortals call it?

THE WAITER: A five-spot.

THE GOOD FAIRY: That's right, a five-spot! . . . Since I've got other things to do than bring you a five-spot every morning, I'm going to give you the whole amount in one lump sum.

THE POOR SLOB: (*Cannot believe his ears.*) In one lump sum! . . . My whole amount in one lump sum! (*He mimes gathering heaps of gold on the table.*) One lump sum!

THE WAITER: (*Stupefied and mimicking the mime.*) One lump sum! You lucky dog! Didn't I tell you something good would happen to you?

THE POOR SLOB: (*To the Good Fairy*) And when will you deliver this little lump?

THE GOOD FAIRY: Aren't you in a hurry, poor slob! I need time to make up your account. Wait just a moment. I'll be right back. (*She exits to the strains of heavenly music.*)

THE WAITER: Wow! Talk about a streak of luck! You're looking for a job and you find . . . a fortune!

THE POOR SLOB: (*Poor-mouthing*) Some fortune! Five francs a day!

THE WAITER: You were stupid not to ask for more.

THE POOR SLOB: How could I know? . . .

THE WAITER: What are you going to do with all that money?

THE POOR SLOB: I'm going to start by buying a hat that's not so red and a coat that's not so green. That'll make a change.

THE WAITER: If I were you, I'd buy a green hat and a red coat, it'd be even more of a change.

THE POOR SLOB: I won't do that. A true gentleman must, above all, refrain from displaying flashy colors in his wardrobe.

THE WAITER: You going to kick up your heels, hmmm?

THE POOR SLOB: (*Shrugging.*) Kick up my heels! High life! Sure, sure! Keep chorus girls! All that on five francs a day! You're crazy, my dear fellow!

THE WAITER: There are chorus girls and chorus girls. Why, I knew some at this one nightclub . . .

THE POOR SLOB: (*Thoughtfully.*) You're right, I was stupid . . . I should have asked for twenty francs. What difference does it make to a good fairy?

THE WAITER: (*Suddenly struck by an idea.*) I know what! Since you're going to get all the dough in one lump sum (*he mimes raking in the gold*), what's stopping you from investing it, instead of stupidly living off the capital?

THE POOR SLOB: I don't know if that would be proper. I'm entitled to five francs, not six.

THE WAITER: Your scruples do you honor; but if I were you, I wouldn't divide it up. The money you're about to get belongs to you. You surely have the right to do what you want with it.

THE POOR SLOB: (*Hesitating.*) I'll think it over.

THE WAITER: Or else, buy a music hall. That'll be lucrative!

THE POOR SLOB: I know what you're after. A music hall where you can warble ballads while you serve the cherry brandy.

THE WAITER: (*Singing.*)

When cherry blossom time returns once more . . .

THE POOR SLOB: (*Stopping him with a gesture.*) Shush! (*Heavenly music.*) Here comes my celestial benefactor. (*Anxiously.*) But where is she keeping the money? She doesn't look bent under the weight of it.

THE WAITER: She's bringing you the amount in large bills.

THE POOR SLOB: Or checks.

THE GOOD FAIRY: Hello again, poor slob! Did you get bored waiting for me?

THE POOR SLOB: Oh no, I was chatting with this gentleman, making plans for the future.

THE GOOD FAIRY: Aha!

THE POOR SLOB: Yes indeed . . . I really haven't made up my mind yet.

THE GOOD FAIRY: Now you can. (*She puts in his hand the sum of seven francs fifty.*) Here you are, poor slob.

THE POOR SLOB: (*Contemplating, dumbfounded, his seven francs fifty.*) What? What in the world is this?

THE GOOD FAIRY: It's your total.

THE POOR SLOB: My total? . . . Seven francs fifty! But you told me you would give it to me all in a lump!

THE GOOD FAIRY: The amount I have handed you, poor slob, represents your sum total.

THE POOR SLOB: (*Obstinately, refusing to understand.*) Seven francs fifty! No, no! You're joking, I'm supposed to get more than that! Tell me you're joking!

THE GOOD FAIRY: Be informed, poor slob, that good fairies never joke.

THE POOR SLOB: Seven francs fifty! . . . But then, if I can count . . . and I *can* count, because I am an accountant by profession, I've got only a day and a half to live?

THE GOOD FAIRY: Alas, poor slob, my power does not extend to prolonging your existence. I am sorry.

THE POOR SLOB: So am I! Another day and a half to live!

THE GOOD FAIRY: Thirty-six hours exactly.

THE POOR SLOB: Not a lot.

THE GOOD FAIRY: Try to resign yourself to it, poor slob.

THE POOR SLOB: Resign! Oh, I'm already resigned! (*Merrily accepting his fate.*) Ooh la la, just watch my dust! (*He tosses his hat in the air and kicks his leg over the table.*) Gather ye rosebuds while ye may! Henceforth my motto shall be: Short and sweet! Bring on those chorus girls. And, for a start, waiter, a Pernod!

THE WAITER: You want the Pernod with anisette?

THE POOR SLOB: No, neat.

THE WAITER: One neat Pernod. (*He starts to sing the angelic chorus from* Faust.)

>Pernod neat, blessèd Pernod.
>Lifts one's soul into the sky.
>On its wings up shall you go.
>To eternal ecstacy on high.

ALL:

>Pernod neat, blessed Pernod
>Lifts one's soul into the sky.

APOTHEOSIS

CURTAIN

GOUDEAU AND HIS BAND OF CHANSONNIERS BEGAN TO HANG OUT at a bar called the *Chat Noir* (Black Cat), which had opened on 18 November 1881 in a former post-office at the foot of Montmartre. It was run by the painter Rodolphe Salis (1851-97), son of a distiller, who intended it as a resort for artists; on Friday nights the Hydropathes and their friends would improvise a private concert. From the start, non-artists would drop by to catch the performance. And so this *cabaret* (tavern), by offering entertainment to a select public, became the pioneer *cabaret artistique*.

At first there was no cover-charge, though Salis insisted on an obligatory beer. The cabaret proved to be too near the public dance halls of the Elysée-Montmartre, and so in 1885 he opened a new Chat Noir in a three-story private house on rue Laval, elegantly furnished with antiques and works of art. There Salis, richly dressed, would treat his guests with an almost chivalric courtesy.

Playing host evolved into a characteristic feature of the cabaret, the *conférencier*. The notion of a *conférence* came from the naturalist theatre, where well-known critics lectured to the public on the slice-of-life it had just seen. Here *conférencier* might be translated by "master of ceremonies" or (in England) "compère," but this does not fully suggest the range of his functions. In addition to introducing the acts, he provided commentary on the audience itself, recited his own songs and jokes, and supplied the unifying mood to link the variegated performance elements of the evening.

The Chat Noir's new locale affected the bohemianism of the atmosphere. Previously, recitation of songs and stories by their creators was the standard entertainment. The music hall ditty had been raised to a true literary form, given to macabre and impudent subject matter. In the new premises, the leading genre was the shadow-play. This may have been initiated by chance when the lights were once turned out on the poet Jules Jouy, and little shadows were cast to amuse the benighted public. In the earliest efforts, the images were cut out of zinc and back-lit. Then the genius of the shadow-play, the painter Henri Rivière, developed elaborate techniques using colored lights and paper and colored glass lit by an oxyhydrogenic apparatus to create illusions of perspective. By 1890 he could display wind and rain effects, clouds scudding across the horizon, looming storms, moon-and sunlight on the water. The shadow-playwrights took advantage of these enhanced techniques: between 1887 and 1896, forty-three plays by nineteen artists were produced.

Of these plays, the acknowledged masterpieces were *Phryné* and *Elsewhere* by the poet Maurice Donnay (1859-1945), who recited them himself in a slow, monotonous tone, extracting all the irony that lurked in the pieces. As Yvette Guilbert recalled, a Donnay dress rehearsal was a well-attended event, accompanied by the same silence one would hear at Bayreuth. The songs that studded these plays came up to the ideal defined by Donnay: "Drastic, audacious, satiric, sneering, mocking, rebellious *chansons*, intoxicated with disrespect for all the powers-that-be and all undeserved manifestations of glory, in continual opposition to stupidity, injustice, and vulgarity." The excerpts from *Elsewhere* given here display the kinds of effects the shadow-play was capable of, and the risqué, Aristophanic satire it expressed.

But "chanoirism" was non-conformist without being truly subversive, for the audience was drawn from the ranks of high society. Indeed, by 1889, when the World Exhibition opened in Paris, the Chat Noir had turned into a tourist attraction, and when Salis's lease ran out in 1897, he closed it.

Elsewhere
(Ailleurs)
A Symbolic Revue in Twenty Scenes
by
Maurice Donnay

for Maître Paul Verlaine

(First produced at the Shadow Theatre of the Chat Noir, 11 November 1891, with designs by Henri Rivière and music by Charles de Sivry)

SCENE ONE

The Institute

(*The scene represents the Seine across from the Institute. The dome of the monument and roofs of the adjacent houses are silhouetted against a sky whose blue background is strewn with an archipelago of clouds which, like snowflakes, drift before a pallid, circular moon. The water reflecting them laps against the black mass of a landing-pier, flanking a solitary flat-bottomed boat downstage. A nearby clock strikes twelve.*)

THE RECITER: The bell tolls midnight. We are on a bank of the Seine, across from the Institute, on a foggy November night. Far off in the distance, on the bridge in the background, a group of students passes by. These youngsters are returning from a banquet at which M. Lévisse told them that they were the hope of France . . . At the moment, the hope of France, dead drunk, is singing smutty choruses:

(*A little student chorus offstage. The music becomes distinct and accompanies the voices.*)

> Let's tighten the screw and keep the screw tight,
> And screw all of them who don't think it right.

(*Repeat. The voices are lost in the distance.*)

THE RECITER: And this is only the beginning. The weather is very cold, chilly blasts are blowing. The sound of a few desperate persons casually throwing themselves in the river does nothing to disturb the selfish dreams of the bourgeois who sleep serenely beneath their warm counterpanes. (*Distant plops, like bodies falling into the Seine, are heard.*) And this is only the beginning. Dark is the night, deep the silence, and deserted Quai Malaquais . . . Voltaire himself has left his pedestal. (*At this moment Voltaire appears.*) When his bronze feet began to fall asleep, he came down onto the flat-bottomed boat and is walking back and forth to keep warm. And while he walks, thoughts, I might even say, satanic thoughts, probably go through his mind, for from time to time a hideous smile brightens this gloomy scene all by itself. (*Lights.*) Fortunately, for by the glow of one of these lights, he notices a man he was about to bump into. Discreetly questioned by Voltaire, this man replies that he is a poet, his name is Terminus, and following an interview committed on him by M. Jules Huret, a benefit performance was instigated against him that rendered him completely destitute; now his declared intention is to jump into the river. He says:

> Alas! I am weary of living!
> The future seems frightfully bleak,
> And I only pile up more misgiving
> When a peek at my past I can sneak.
>
> Sweet nothingness, Paradise lost,
> Oh, when will you waft us away,

And in pledge for our living's high cost
With a well-earned respite us repay?

Ah! cyclical reincarnation,
How banal I find nature's laws,
That every effect in creation
Must invariably follow its cause.

To say what's been said by each mortal,
To tell time by that same old clock,
To hear at each door and each portal
The same everlasting ''Knock, knock!''

To lean on the same old zinc bars
By the same empty bottles untempted;
To find all the ways to the stars
By white-haired old gents were pre-empted.

If to beauty and love you aspire,
The brunettes all have contrary minds!
And the blondes will too often spit fire,
There's something to say for both kinds.

After all, we poor strummers of lyres
Come second to lovers who pay,
We're scavengers down in the mire
For fag-ends of smiles, you might say.

Besides, after singing the graces
Of iris-hued ladies, to wind
Up with night-crawlers' whorrible faces,
Can drive a man out of his mind!

You dream of adventures exciting,
Of castles in azure-blue climes
And marvelous whirlwinds inviting
To the stars' stately dance in waltz-time.

And then you fall back, weak as jelly,
To find yourself wobbling away
In a belly dance with empty belly
Before an unyielding buffet.

I've spent the day walking the city,
Like the hero of . . . I can't be sure . . .

It's aphasia . . . My plight's not pretty!
But this is my ultimate tour.

Funny thing, I can feel no regret;
It may be my brain-sickness which
Makes the city seem empty and yet
It's cold as a sonuvabitch,

The atmosphere's filthy with sleaze:
The boulevards fill me with pain:
I've done all the bridges and quais,
All I've left to do now is the Seine.

And he leaps into it. And by an urgent power of suggestion,
which, we admit, is almost improbable, Voltaire leaps in too.

SCENE TWO

Cape Magi

(*In a green atmosphere, rocks tumble tormented towards the sea.*)

THE RECITER: Down at the bottom of the Seine, Voltaire and Terminus met with a tunnel they threaded their way through like a
pearl on a string. How is it done? Nobody knows: no one will
ever know. Be that as it may, at this moment they are on the
verge of a trip through fantastic countries, an extraordinary
voyage, and it will really be pure Jules Verne, if not Shakespeare
or, better put, "the Bard." At that moment, tiny, they travel to
the tops of gigantic and jagged mountains: this is Cape Magi, a
fearsome spot for the uninitiate; but fortunately Terminus knows
the esoteric doctrine, and the two travelers can proceed without
being too troubled. From time to time however, beings or rather,
invisible principles well-known by the name of larvae, whisper as
they pass:
OFFSTAGE VOICES: (*Orchestra: Ballet of the Sylphes, from* The
Damnation of Faust.) Do you sleep soundly, Voltaire? Do you
sleep soundly, Voltaire?
THE RECITER: Voltaire is annoyed; but Terminus explains that
these are no doubt larvae from the *Chat Noir,* larvae which, as
everyone knows, show no respect to anything, and the best

response is to laugh. Voltaire laughs.

(*During this scene, the orchestra has played rather infernal music: Voltaire's laugh is indicated by a sequence of shrill, hurried chords.*)

SCENE THREE

Constantine Bay

(*The shores of a tranquil sea; slender, bosky trees; a blue sky in which clouds, scalloped by the moon, drift and assume strange shapes.*)

THE RECITER: On leaving the jagged mountains, Voltaire and Terminus reach the strand of a calm sea where everything is restful, cool, serene, and poetic. Barely have their feet trod this blessed sod when they suddenly feel much better: this is Constantine Bay. The landscape conduces towards reverie. Leaning against the slender trunk of a plane-tree, they watch the sky, and the sight of the sky, the moon, and clouds inspires tender thoughts in the poet Terminus. Far from hiding them, he immediately puts them in verse and sets them to music, thus composing a ballad. He sings:

When the evening's sweet perfume,
Like dark incense from a tomb
Rises from the earth's brown womb,
In reverie we stare
At the clouds the windy air
Hurries scudding past the moon.

Bathed in its weird pallid rays,
At the cobalt sky we gaze,
And with optics strange we see,
Towers, temples, piles,
Reed-bedizened isles,
A fantastic argosy,

Warriors gigantic,
Sphinxes, monsters frantic,
Or lustful women taut,

Naked limbs distorting,
Hornèd goats cavorting,
Madonnas rapt in thought.

The poets go on dreaming,
The clouds go on unseaming,
The crazy, sudden shower
Has drenched us through and through,
And made sure that we withdrew
From our safe ivory tower.

(*While he sings, the clouds sail through the sky, taking the forms he mentions: in the last verse, the clouds resolve into rain.*)

SCENE FOUR

The Outskirts

THE RECITER: And they keep going: a milestone, on which are inscribed the words: *"Elsewhere, 6 kilometers"* informs them that they are approaching their goal, while numerous signboards all forbidding something instruct them that they are about to enter a free state: "No Bill-Posting, No Smoking, Hunting by License Only, Hunting Restricted, Road Obstructed, Fresh Paint—Don't Touch, Do Not Put Your Head, Arms, Legs, or Anything Else Outside!" There is also a toll-house and a police station as befits a civilized community.

[*In the next scenes, Terminus and Voltaire meet with Adolphe, the Sad Young Man, and learn that his mother has suffered prenatal influence from hideous municipal statues. They encounter a racy music hall singer named Sorrel, a pun on* l'oseille *(sorrel) and* osée *(daring). They then enter the forest of the poets, and a poetic competition evokes a terrifying thunderstorm, ending in a gorgeous rainbow. As Voltaire and Terminus pray at this Holy Hour of Absinthe, Part One ends.*]

PART TWO

SCENE ELEVEN

The Clearing

(*Amid the tall trees of a dreamy clearing, Voltaire and Terminus appear first very small, then they disappear and return ever larger and larger in proportion to their approaching the forestage. Very gentle music which is not a march but almost a lullaby accompanies their walk, an impalpable glide.*)

THE RECITER: They make their way in silence.

SCENE TWELVE

Exhausted Eros

(*A pagan temple: a cypress wood beneath a pearl-gray and mauve sky, twilight. A stooped young man emerges from the temple: drooping wings are attached to his shoulders: he is Eros.*)

THE RECITER: And they go on seeking the causes of Adolphe's sadness. They arrive at the Cycle of Love. And in an attenuated landscape, beneath a pastel-colored sky, they notice a ruined temple surrounded by black cypresses. Love himself comes to meet the noble visitors leaning on his bow as on a crutch, and oh so pale! and ah so wasted! and ah how weary!!! And Voltaire, addressing him: ''Are you indeed Eros, son of Mars and Venus?'' And he replies:

The deity who pierced men's hearts,
Born 'neath Greece's sunny sky,
Who triumphed with his light-fledged darts,
I'm not that god, not I;

No son of Mars the warrior bold
And Venus of the charming scandals
Nor Zephyr with the ringlets gold
And Iris of unsullied sandals.

I am the fruit of a quick affair
In a backstairs slum bohemia,
'Twixt a bookie with red body hair
And a hooker with anemia.

I'm older than you would suppose,
For I was born worn out and jaded
On the petal-bed of a crumbling rose:
Like the faded rose, Eros is faded.

I am not the god who drives
Lovers, to the river fled,
To cancel out their blighted lives,
Or helps fond couples into bed;

The god of happy wedded bliss,
Whose torches light up nuptial rooms;
Who staggers virgins with a kiss
From handsome, ardent young bridegrooms.

The God who sows and procreates,
Safeguards, as his vocation,
The ancient law that validates
The world's rejuvenation.

A lesser mission is my vaunt:
To pedophiles I tender
Young waiters from the restaurant
And Boy Scouts, pink and slender.

The matches I make, you might guess,
Do not increase the birth-rate much;
I tend the lesbian caress
Of women whom no man may touch.

Divide and conquer, that's my way,
And for each smutty act
That seeks the shadows, I just say:
Sterility and tact.

I am blond: my emerald eyes
Get nervous types all flustered;
I teach mistresses to disguise
When men can't cut the mustard.

Like serpents, I can twist with ease,
In lore of perfumes I'm well-read,
And I have secret strategies
To raise one's senses from the dead.

Of tingling tawse I know the trick
For impotents, that sorry brood,
And to inflict the right pinprick
To stimulate their sluggish blood.

I am the morphine addict's god,
Who seeks the new and strange,
Sophisticates by me are awed,
Their brain-cells I derange.

I'm older than you would suppose,
For I was born worn out and jaded
On the petal-bed of a crumbling rose;
Like the faded rose, Eros is faded!

SCENE THIRTEEN

The Lesbians

(*A field of orchids which slowly undulate, while above the flowers voluptuous naked women, embracing like lovers in Dante, pass in a sky changing from green to blue to pink.*)

THE RECITER: Adolphe wanted to love; he wanted to love, did Adolphe; but he did not find any women, sentimentally, at any rate . . . or scarcely . . . And in the Cycle of Love, the poets meet the Lesbians. They come to a field of bizarre, unnerving orchids, which raise their exaggerated stamens to the sky. And above the tall flowers which undulate like waves beneath the wind of their flight, women pass, come and go, whirl, waltz, spin, leap, in each other's embrace for eternity, women who indulge in blameworthy tribadiddling, as M. Bergerat would say, if he were Alsatian. Now they pass, embracing, through an old rose sky, the lovers of Times Gone By and those of Already, and there are Mlle de Maupin and the Girl with the Golden Eyes. And also Baby Orgasm and Wax-Candle Rose. And then too Jo and Zo and Lo

. . . and Ro and Fo and No, why not? Terminus names some of the creatures of our time as they pass: Duchess of A. . . , Marquise of B. . . , Countess of C. . . , Baroness of D. . . , for there are great ladies; there are even crowned heads, these loves being reputed so rare, literary, and aristocratic. True, their numbers also include young ladies from the Moulin-Rouge and shoestitchers; but no matter, they do not look so closely. Now, in innumerable couples, they pass, embracing, vertiginous, and the wind of their whirling makes the tall orchids undulate like waves.

SCENE FOURTEEN

The Importunate Androgyne

(*A gallery lined with statues, among them Pradier's Sappho, the Venus de Milo, Falguière's Diana, and also a Cleopatra.*)

THE RECITER: And still in the Cycle of Love, having turned leftwards, Terminus and Voltaire come to a gallery lined with statues. There is Sappho, there is Venus, there is Diana, there is Cleopatra, there are others you cannot see. They think they are in a museum and prepare to look without touching, when they see a woman come in, followed by a long greyhound. "Isn't that Lady Jane Greyhound?" Voltaire asks wittily. "No," says his companion, "that's the importunate androgyne." And indeed it is the importunate androgyne, with its little hat, its little collar, its English tie, its man's shirt, its tailored jacket, and its umbrella-shaped fur dress. It arrives humming a favorite refrain with a casual air, a refrain from the good old days that our fathers sang.

(*Tune from* La Périchole.)

Ah, women, ah, women, there's nothing else but
So long as the world keeps yearning,
So long as the earth keeps turning,
Ah, women, there's nothing else but.

At present the importunate androgyne is in a quandary. It is weary of mistresses of flesh and blood in whom it finds no doubt not enough consistency, and, a new though second-rate Pygmalioness, it is trying to animate marble. It approaches Venus and makes a troubling declaration to her. But, just at the moment when it believes its prayers have been answered and that, following the advice of M. Legouvé Senior, it is about to fall at the feet of the sex to which it owes its mother, Hercules answers it and says:

> Oh malfeasant monster, take heed of this story,
> And keep it preserved in your feeble memóry;
> I'd not, I believe, reached the age of eighteen,
> A sapling, a stripling, in short, I was green,
> When the old king of Thespies, now ancient and weak,
> Called me to him, and said, though he barely could speak:
> A lion is eating Amphytrion's sheep,
> You must fight him and kill him, so we get some sleep.
> Now this mighty monarch of daughters had fifty,
> Count'em, fifty, and trust me, were they ever nifty!
> And since I was spending the night there, why not?
> They noiselessly visited me in my cot,
> Impassioned and nude, they put up no defense,
> I knew each one in turn, in the Biblical sense.

"Oh! Oh!" goes Voltaire. The importunate androgyne recoils in horror; but does not consider itself beaten; it takes more than that. It moves rapidly past the Diana whose reproduction is forbidden, and makes Cleopatra a troubling declaration, the same, for it has only one, its brain being uncomplicated; but at the moment when it is about to kneel before the Queen of Egypt, the bull that possessed Pasiphaë rises erect before it, his horns rampant. This time the importunate androgyne confesses itself vanquished; it runs off in despair. Voltaire and Terminus are quite pleased. It is the revenge of Nature. They notice just now that they are capable of siring someone; they don't think that a bad thing.

SCENE FIFTEEN

The Black Mass

(The ruins of a temple. Under the somber arcades a crowd of Satanists is moving in a strange Sabbath: they are roasting little *children on big bonfires; demons grimace behind the pillars. Strange music: fifes, kettle-drums. The unleashed orchestra pulls out its gongs.)*

THE RECITER: And still in the Cycle of Love, having turned right this time for a change, Voltaire and Terminus arrive underneath the arches of a dilapidated and sinister temple. There disheveled women and drunken men are stirring, seeking, pursuing, making brutish love: these are Satanists, possessed by a terrifying demon of lust. They rejoice, like the late Dolmancé whose story you have all read, at least I like to think so, in uniting sacrilege to lechery . . . It's nasty stuff. All these people feed exclusively on hosts dipped in the blood of incestuous lovers or at the very least adulterers . . . Who would have thought it. Seated on a big stone in the guise of an altar, Canon Docre, horrible, grimacing, presides over the orgiastic scenes whose aim is to parody the ceremonies of the Holy Mass, hence the name Black Mass bestowed on these practices. Suddenly a young girl, still almost a virgin, strikes a gong. *(Gong sound.)* That is the signal: the horrors are about to begin. *(Suddenly, the scene grows dark and becomes impenetrable.)* ''But I can't see anything!'' Voltaire timidly remarks. ''Of course not,'' Terminus replies judiciously, ''since it's a *black* mass.'' ''In that case,'' Voltaire says with some regret, ''it was hardly worth the trouble of making our mouths water, so to speak.''

[*They come to the banks of the Nile, and the story of Moses in the bulrushes is told as a prelude to anti-Semitic jokes about the origin of stockbrokers, which lead in turn to an episode at the ruined stock exchange. This ends in an image of Christ between two tycoons. Then there is a parody of chauvinism and cheap militarism, followed by a pageant of socialism, and finally the interior of Notre Dame Cathedral. As Voltaire returns to his pedestal before daybreak, Terminus in a final poem confesses his faith in better times to come.*]

Translator's Notes

Jules Huret was the most famous interviewer in Parisian journalism.
Auguste Emile Bergerat, poet, playwright, and critic.

James Pradier had long been deceased, but *Jean Falguiéres* was still a professor at the Ecole des Beaux-Arts.

Mlle de Maupin and *The Girl with the Golden Eyes* are works on sapphic themes by Théophile Gautier and Honoré de Balzac, respectively.

''Fall at the feet of that sex to which you owe your mother'' was a line from *Gabriel Legouvé's* poem ''What Women Deserve,'' a line so silly it became proverbial.

Dolmancé is the arch-libertine of Marquis de Sade's *Histoire de Juliette*.

Canon Docre is the evil priest in Joris-Karl Huysman's novel of Satanism *Là-bas*, published the year before Donnay's playlet.

ALTHOUGH SHE SELDOM PERFORMED IN THE *CABARET ARTISTIQUE*, Yvette Guilbert (1867-1944) had a profound influence on the genre. Once a milliner, she gained stage experience in the French provinces, where she was often whistled and laughed off the stage, for her looks were totally out of fashion. The usual music hall singer was a plump beauty with opulent curves and deep cleavage; Guilbert was scrawny, red-haired, chinless, and long-nosed. She seemed doomed to obscurity, when in 1891 she found in a quai bookstall a volume of poems by Léon Xanrof (1867-1953).

Xanrof (his real name Fourneau—oven—he translated into Latin as Fornax and then shuffled the letters) was a lawyer turned songwriter, who hung out at the Chat Noir. His nonsense tune, *The Cab*, had been introduced by the well-known Félicia Mallet with no special acclaim. Guilbert sang it "between clenched teeth" at the Moulin Rouge dance hall, half an hour before the public was admitted. The critic for *Gil Blas* happened to hear her, and praised her to the skies. *The Cab* became her theme song and Xanrof one of her favorite purveyors.

Guilbert then enjoyed a meteoric rise to fame at the *Divan japonais*, a low-ceilinged literary café where, despite the name, the décor was Chinese. It had been founded by Jehan Sarrazin, an olive dealer with a passion for poetry. Most of the Hydropathe crew began to write songs for Guilbert, and in 1892 the Chat Noir suspended its rules of all-male performance by making her a member and letting her sing there. Through Guilbert, the songs from Donnay's shadow plays were also introduced to a wider public.

Classified as a *diseuse*, Gulbert turned music hall singing into a subtle art not just by a discriminating choice of material but by her nuanced, suggestive mode of recitation. She had only the "ghost of a voice," according to the composer Gounod, but her impeccable diction, ability to suggest hidden obscenities, and an actor's sureness of timing turned every song into a one-act play. Guilbert's style remained idiosyncratic, but provided a model for performers in the intimate new ambience of the cabaret.

The Cab
(Le Fiacre)
1892
by
Léon Xanrof

A cab went jolting through the night,
Clip-clop, clip-clop, gidyap! hop-la!
A cab went jolting through the night,
 The horse was gray, the coachman white.

The blinds were down, but could not hide,
Clip-clop, clip-clop, gidyap! hop-la!
The blinds were down, but could not hide
 The sound of kissing from inside.

"Léon!" a woman's voice did say,
Clip-clop, clip-clop, gidyap! hop-la!
"Léon!" a woman's voice did say,
 "That hurts! Please take off your pince-nez!"

An agèd gent was passing by,
Clip-clop, clip-clop, gidyap! hop-la!
An agèd gent was passing by
 And cried, "Why . . . I could swear that I

Can hear my spouse's voice somewhere."
Clip-clop, clip-clop, gidyap! hop-la!
Can hear my spouse's voice somewhere."
 He rushed into the thoroughfare.

His foot slipped in a pile of slush,
  Clip-clop, clip-clop, gidyap! hop-la!
His foot slipped in a pile of slush,
  Crack! the cab crushed him to mush!

The woman left the cab and said,
  Clip-clop, clip-clop, gidyap! hop-la!
The woman left the cab and said,
  "Lucky us, my husband's dead!"

"No more giving him the slip!
  Clip-clop, clip-clop, gidyap! hop-la!
"No more giving him the slip!
  Don't be stingy with the tip!"

ONE OF THE CHANSONNIERS WHO MADE A REPUTATION AT THE first Chat Noir was Aristide Bruant (1851-1925), who wrote its theme song:

By light of the moon
On Montmartre's height,
I search for fortune
At the Chat Noir tonight.

He also served as a conférencier on occasion. But his crude manner and familiarity sorted ill with Salis's more courtly style, and when the Chat Noir moved, Bruant took over the old premises, reopening them as *Le Mirliton* (The Reed-Pipe). There, accompanied by the pianist-composer Paul Carrière and two men who joined him in the choruses, Bruant in his sombrero, red scarf, and boots would insult his audiences. As late-comers arrived, they would be greeted with ''All right, you dumb bunny, park your guts next to that lady . . . And you, you big salami, squeeze your carcass between those two who don't even know why they're laughing like a couple of idiots!'' And if they left early: ''So long! Both those virgins belong to you? The gent keeps two pieces of ass on hand to make sure he gets two-timed. Good night, ladies, make him happy!'' The chorus to one song ran, ''The customers are always swine!'' Essentially these customers were the same high-toned crowd that went to the Chat Noir; Francis Carco noted, ''Last night these very same spectators visited Salis who called them, 'My Lords, Gentlemen, Your High-nesses,' and they were happy. Tonight they visit Bruant who calls them names of fish, amphibians, or ruminants, according to sex, and they are happier still.''

Bruant's fare was more proletarian, for he sang of the lives of the apache or hooligan and the slut who loved him. His bourgeois guest had the thrill of slumming and hearing exotic slang without any danger, for Bruant was only superficially naturalistic—as one critic put it, populist without being popular. His songs of the *Lumpen-proletariat* are difficult to translate since they rely so much on underworld cant, Parisian place-names, and feminine rhymes. The following, two of Bruant's most powerful numbers, make a stab at it.

Jules Jouy was once in the country with his girlfriend when he heard a chorus of birdsong. "What would Bruant say if he heard all those birds singing," he asked Marinette. "Bruant would say . . . Shut yer traps, I'm gonna sing!" was her reply. More overtly political than Bruant, Jouy (1855-97), a jeweler and painter on porcelain, began writing music hall songs, including some for Yvette Guilbert, in his spare time. He went through the usual progression from the Hydropathes to the Chat Noir, and then in 1895 founded the *Chien-Noir* (Black Dog) to house refugees from the older cabaret. Jouy was no musician but his diction was trenchant and he accompanied himself on the piano with a tinkling chord repeated over and over.

Throwing himself into politics, he founded two papers, the *Cri du Peuple* (Cry of the People, 1886-88) and *Le Parti Ouvrier* (Worker's Party, 1888-89) which printed a song each day devoted to that day's events: Jouy's mordant ballads concerned ministerial crises, strikes, capital punishment, alcoholism, and martyrs of the Commune. *The Song of the Working Girl*, based on a news item, made the hearers tremble when he sang it. Paranoid and paralytic, he spent his last two years in a madhouse.

Out in the Street
(Dans la Rue)
by
Aristide Bruant

I dunno if I come from Grenel-le,
From Montmartre or from La Chapel-le,
From here or somewhere else on the map,
All I know's a crowd of runnin' feet
Found me lying on a pile of crap
Out in the street.

I guess it's more'n likely that my pa
Had no formal intro to my ma
Who never met my dear old dad:
He got plowed, so plowed her a treat,
And then she knew that she'd been had,
Out in the street.

I ain't had no folks o' me own or that,
Just a pack of l'il snotnose brats,
So when the time came to get spliced,
The broad I shacked up with walked a beat
And hustled nights, at a good price,
Out in the street.

My missus was a l'il blond teaser,
With a kisser like the Mona Lisa,
Pointed tits and round bum on the lass,
This dame was stacked real nice an' neat

Like them statues that flash their ass
Out in the street.

She made me happy as a pig in muck! . . .
But one fine night we ran out o' luck:
The vice squad stuck her in the jug
And, while she had to face the heat,
I went lookin' for guys I could mug and slug
Out in the street.

So now what'm I supposed to do!
Want me to go to work? Sez you!
I cou'n't do't . . . I was never taught . . .
Guess I gotta steal or kill t' eat . . .
Big deal! Screw it, I won't get caught . . .
Out in the street.

Who the hell cares! Long live my pals!
Long live the crooks and the workin' gals! . . .
Some day soon I'm gonna come a cropper
And a crowd'll show up with runnin' feet
To see my neck beneath the chopper,
Out in the street.

The Guillotine
(*A la Roquette*)
1889
by
Aristide Bruant

As I shout out these words, my guts
Quake, past controlling.
And as you read 'em my head juts
Through a round op'ning.
Since midnight I've been wide awake,
Toinette, poor darling,
I hear the kind of noise they make
When guillotining.

The president refused to sign
A pardon for me,
They'd think that he was out o' line
If I went scot-free.
If pardons grew on ev'ry tree,
Law'd have no meaning!
Heads gotta roll occas'nally
By guillotining!

The sun is lighting up the sky,
The night is past now;
Those gents will soon be coming by,
Day breaks too fast now.
Outside distinctly I can hear
The wild mob keening,

It wants to raise the fun'ral cheer
For guillotining.

That don't faze me, hey, what the heck.
What gets me iced here
Is that before they cut my neck
My collar's sliced here.
When picturing the shears' cold blade
Through shirt careening,
I feel real chilly and afraid,
At guillotining.

I gotta tough it out, with grace
Show I'm no faker.
No one'll say I couldn't face
The widow-maker.
No stage fright then, no nerve attack,
Just watch me preening
Before I sneeze into the sack
When guillotining.

The Working Girl
(*Fille d'ouvriers*)
c. 1886
by
Jules Jouy

"However, the foreman confessed to all the charges in his indictment; . . . separated from his wife, and wanting more than life in common-law wedlock with another woman, he also took as his mistress a young girl of twenty who worked in his shop."

—*Cri du Peuple,* The St-Denis Scandal

Pale or rosy, dark or fair,
  Baby bubble,
Born in tears, she greets the air,
  Meat for trouble.
Thumb in mouth and runny nose,
  Unwashed reject,
Like a mushroom up she grows,
  Meat for neglect!

At fifteen, the factory beckons;
  That way trudging,
Same old grind at ev'ry second,
  Meat for drudging.
Of strong stock, away she'll pine.
  If she's sweet,

She's raped after closing-time,
  Boss's meat.

The rot sets in, advances far,
  Nothing to eat,
She finds a job behind a bar,
  Customers' meat.
On ever lower rungs she sticks,
  Ashamed but beat,
At two francs she's turning tricks,
  Meat for the street.

Older, sliding down non-stop . . .
  Life's not a lark.
She'll get run in by a cop,
  Meat for a nark;
Or else, at home, ''no yellow card,''
  She's still for sale;
The time she'll serve is one year's hard,
  Meat for the jail.

A wasting plague attacks her bones.
  Trembling, infirm,
In charity ward she lies and groans,
  Meat for interns.
Then, at last, she's drained the cup,
  No more transits.
Now she's dead they cut her up,
  Meat for lancets.

Bosses! pack of sybarites,
  When your gullets
At our guns gape wide in fright,
  Meat for bullets,
So every passing dog can piss
  Upon your faces,
We'll leave your carrion as it is,
  Meat leaves no traces!

HOLLAND WAS UNPROMISING GROUND FOR PLANTING A CABARET: Calvinistic, ridden with taboos about sex, morality, unsavoury social conditions, the royal family and the armed services, the Dutch Establishment used legislation, censorship, newspaper campaigns, and social pressure to suppress satire. Artists were seen as *agents provocateurs*.

The first Dutch cabaret performances, imitating Bruant, were one-man shows offending the audience. Eduard Jacobs (1868-1914), known as the "minstrel of the dungheap," came from a family of musicians and trained as a diamond cutter. But from 1891 to 1894 he played piano in Paris at the Moulin Rouge, accompanying, among others, the Petomane who kept his audience in stitches by farting popular tunes. In August 1895 Jacobs opened the first Amsterdam cabaret in the disreputable slum De Pijp (The Pipe); he sang his own songs or translations of French numbers, and if, when Jacobs passed the hat, an audience member failed to come across, he might get a punch in the head. Jacobs sang in the vernacular, his usual subjects prostitution (which obsessed him), alcoholism, street crime, rape and murder, abortion and domestic violence, in short, the "naturalist" agenda, winning him the label "the Zola of song."

Now famous, he played in The Hague and even worked big halls like the Concertgebouw, but the police hounded him from his own premises in 1904 by intimidating his customers. The complaint was his reliance on "morbid songs." To recoup his losses, Jacobs toured the Dutch East Indies from 1912 to 1914, but wore himself out and died nine months after his return to Holland.

The Whore Fleet

(De hoerenvloot)

c. 1895

by

Eduard Jacobs

If you let your eyes roam freely
  in the underworld of tarts,
you can't help but get to thinking
  about other counterparts.
So I did a little research
  among sluts big and petite,
now I'll sing you my conclusions,
  simply titled "The Whore Fleet."
          (repeat last two lines)

Comes an inexperienced floozy
  To a dive of great repute,
She must learn how to be choosey,
  what goes over, what's no good.
But the Madam there will teach her,
  she's a veteran who's hip,
though a wreck no hand would sail on
  still of use as "Training Ship."
          (repeat last two lines)

Know what metaphoric thingy
  I would call a love true-blue?
I would say it was a dinghy
  'cause it fits a one-man crew.

But for mistresses a-plenty,
  symbols stand in low esteem.
They may start out as a dinghy
  But plough on like a "Trireme."
                (*repeat last two lines*)

On the corner of dark alleys
  down there by the meanest stews,
you will find the kind of hookers
  give no quarter, stick like glue.
They show every curse of Venus
  in plain detail on their map.
There's a ship "In Quarantine" now,
  leave her be or get the clap!
                (*repeat last two lines*)

Heard a tootsie swear just lately
  that she wasn't the town slut.
And it's true, she won't shack up with
  any penniless ol' mutt.
Flash your cash and she's your lady,
  into bed she'll climb, you bet.
Well, a warship of that nature's
  Called an "Iron-clad Corvette."
                (*repeat last two lines*)

See two young colonial tommies,
  as in harbor dives you range,
Picking up a red-hot momma,
  who divests them of their change.
She divides her favors fairly
  till no sign-up money's left,
then this "Military Transport"
  sends them back to camp bereft!
                (*repeat last two lines*)

A governess with prissy manners
  Is reputed to be tops.
Alternating in her boudoir
  First comes sonny, then comes Pops.
Wifie too spends pleasant hours
  Taking French from Mademoiselle.

Such a prim and proper phony's
  Called a ''Clipper,'' suits her well.
      (repeat last two lines)

She was once a frisky chippy
  but she's long been past her prime.
Now she's poxy, old, and ugly,
  on her soul she spends her time.
Peddling tracts, she prowls the streets still,
  near the church you'll see her lope,
That whore's named in my flotilla
  ''Missionary-ship Good Hope.''
      (repeat last two lines)

The Bastard
(De smeerlap)
1895
by
Eduard Jacobs

Ladies and gentlemen, as usual I'll sing you some songs from my own repertoire. But for those who aren't familiar with the realistic intentions of my verses, I had better begin with a brief explanation. I sing about general conditions and specific people and I do it in a way that strikes many people as strange and daring. That's because I use words which you all use every day, or at least quite frequently, when you're among friends. I do the same thing here, but I do it in public. The reason is that I want to break with what is supposed to be decent and proper and won't allow ordinary life to call a spade a spade. Now it makes no sense to me why I should use in public a language different from the one I'd use in private. This concerns the form of my cabaret songs. But I think I also better mention something about their content. When you become acquainted with some of my pieces you'll notice that they have a serious moral basis. That's the reason I totally reject the notion that my verses are immoral. After this brief introduction, ladies and gentlemen, which was quite necessary for many of you, I will first present you with ''The Bastard.''

She loved him from love's brimming cup,
She didn't know he'd knocked her up,
Didn't understand her sick condition.
God damn him to perdition.
She wrote a lengthy note to him,

Dared call herself his poor victim.
The bastard ignored her petition.
God damn him to perdition.
She told his dad what he had done,
He paid her, though he blamed his son.
Her silence was his one condition.
God damn him to perdition.
She's brought to the delivery room
And there she dies that afternoon.
The bastard sent flow'rs in contrition.
God damn him to perdition.

THE STEP FROM ROMANTIC STREET-SINGING TO PROFESSIONAL cabaret in Holland was taken by Jean-Louis Pisuisse (1880-1927), who came of a musical family descended from Huguenot refugees. He started as a journalist, but began performing cabaret in 1907 in the Dutch East Indies where he made his reputation. The versatile Pisuisse performed in French, English, and German, as well as Dutch; he ran his own ensemble, the *Intiem Theater*, in the resort town of Scheveningen, appearing as conférencier and loquacious songster. Many of his songs are known by heart by the Dutch to this day. Twice married, and, like Jacobs, an inveterate womanizer, Pisuisse loved to sing about women as sex objects. It came as no surprise when he was shot and killed by another of his mistress's lovers on Rembrandt Square in the heart of Amsterdam.

I Sing of Ladies' Footwear
(Nu vil ik van damesschoentjes zingen)
1917
by
Jean-Louis Pisuisse

Ladies and Gentlemen, most esteemed gentlemen and dearly beloved ladies.

The subject of my next talk is the most interesting and most charming one a talk can desire, that is to say Woman. Now I don't mean women in general, because that subject can't be dealt with in a single talk, but I'm referring to one little detail that pertains to her. For it is woman who rules the world, rules life, hence quite possibly rules the song of life as well. Quite so. If you want to write and sing songs you first have to apply yourself to the study of She who plays the most important role in songs (and everywhere else): Her Majesty Woman.

That's what I did, and let me recommend it to you gentlemen— that is if you still qualify—because woman is a most wonderful course of study. Rather expensive, it's true. I've lost my hair and my money in the process. But very pleasant. All my life I've sung about women's hearts, women's eyes, women's dresses, women's hats, women's bags . . . and now I want to sing about women's shoes, because the great variety of her footwear demonstrates the versatility of the female character all the more clearly.

At dawn, when the sun rises in yon russet eastern sky, woman too arises from her couch . . . and puts her slippers on. As far as I'm concerned, I prefer those slippers known as mules, you know, cute little mules with those clattering heels? It's a preference I picked up in the Indies. Now if I may give the married gentlemen here some good advice: the next time you're looking for a present for your wife, and you want to get one that you can enjoy too, give her a pair of those mules with the clattering heels . . . you'll be able to hear her coming . . . which can have its advantages!

Around noon a woman gets rid of her slippers and pulls on her bootees. Well, I'd better say: boots. Because they've got bigger and bigger, no, not around, but lengthwise. The reason why women's boots are getting longer is because their skirts are getting shorter. I'm sure you remember that skirts have gone through a period of getting shorter and shorter, and I mean *short*, folks! They got so short I got scared to death and wondered, ''Where's this gonna end?'' But the ladies, they're so very clever, for the shorter the skirts got, the longer the boots got. And we were nowhere after all!

Now it's in those boots that the ladies go shopping in the afternoon, head downtown, or take tea together. But when six o'clock rolls around and they've got to get ready for the evening's conquests, then off come the boots and on go the shoes. And that's really what I want to talk about: those shoes. Those petite, innocent-looking shoes have a mysterious attraction that even a sober and sedate man like myself—did I say that: sober and sedate?—even a man like me becomes very attracted to them. Because that cute little thing, that graceful, elegant, impractical piece of furniture on stilts is so adorable that it will cause the greatest intellectual to fall to pieces. I'll give you proof in a moment. Even *I* never wrote more important lyrics than these about a lady's shoe. I saw that shoe one evening in one of the few places still left of what used to be Amsterdam's glorious night-life, it was in one of those establishments where our capital's sophisticated entertainment reaches unheard-of heights. Of course I seldom frequent places like that, unless to educate myself so I can pass that knowledge on to you.

As I said, the lyrics are mine, the music is by Max Tak, and the shoe in question probably belonged to someone else.

(*Sung.*)

We men have to lay the blame on our own sex
—Ladies, don't hear and despise us—
It's we ourselves who put your foot on our necks
And let you control and chastise us.

There's times we rebel, but we soon come around
For a smile or a kiss overdue,
And we grovel and kowtow, our face to the ground,
To kiss your patent-leather sweet shoe!

A shadow-play performed at the Chat Noir. Drawing by Alfred Le Petit.

The antique interior of the Chat Noir, from Paris Pittoresque, *1885.*

A caricature of Rodolphe Salis by Charles Léandre, 1895. He is reciting a poem about one of Napoleon's campaigns to a shadow-play in the background.

Yvette Guilbert at her dressing table.

Caricature of Maurice Donnay with the Chat Noir itself.

Caricature of Léon Xanrof by
B. Moloch. The Cab *is in*
the lower right-hand corner.

Lithograph by Toulouse-
Lautrec of Aristide Bruant
at Les Ambassadeurs.

Interior of the Mirliton, by Steinlen.

Caricature of Jules Jouy performing at the Black Dog, by Alfred Le Petit.

Eduard Jacobs at the piano. A photograph pasted on the cover of the sheet music to his song "De Bankiertjes."

Caricature of Jean-Louis Pisuisse.

II

THE ARTISTIC CABARET
IN
GERMANY

1897-1910

SINCE THE EIGHTEENTH CENTURY BERLIN HAD KNOWN TAVERNS where artists congregated. The most famous, perhaps, was *Zum Schwarzen Ferkel* (At the Sign of the Black Piglet), a hangout for aesthetic fugitives like the Swedish dramatist August Strindberg, the Norwegian painter Edvard Munch, and the Polish writer Stanisław Przybyszewski.

But the first deliberate attempt at a German *cabaret artistique* was the brainchild of Baron Ernst von Wolzogen (1855-1934), who ran an Academic-Dramatic Association in Berlin. The son of a Prussian aristocrat and an Englishwoman, Wolzogen was acquainted with developments in variety art outside Germany and with the work of Otto Julius Bierbaum (1865-1910). Bierbaum, a philandering poet and novelist, always anxious to unsettle the bourgeoisie, had proposed an artistic ennobling of variety theatre in his novel *Stilpe*. The disreputable, drunken, over-honest journalist who is the title character sets forth a program for such a music hall; and, in a premonition of Wedekind, himself performs in a cheap suburban variety theatre.

Wolzogen, following Bierbaum's example, published some elegant music hall lyrics, and proposed that an *Überbrettl* be opened at the Art Nouveau Exhibition in Darmstadt in 1900. The term *Überbrettl* was an amalgam of Nietzsche's *Übermensch*, or Superman, and the popular term for a small stage: an English equivalent might be Supergaff. When the Darmstadt project failed to materialize, Wolzogen opened his *Buntes Theater* (Motley Theatre) in Berlin on 17 January 1901.

The Motley Theatre was meant to be a copy of the Chat Noir, although Wolzogen had to avoid political satire because of state censorship. Another important difference was that Wolzogen, as he said himself, was ''never a bohemian''; he did not choose to put himself on a familiar footing with his guests. His chief aims were ''to pull some rotten old teeth'' and to ''bring minor art to a more appreciable and subtle form for fastidious tastes,'' just as Bierbaum hoped for ''all art and all life to be reborn by way of the music hall.''

The founders of the Überbrettl sought to invigorate modern art by refining the vitality of the popular variety stage, whose attraction lay in its vigor, geniality, and adversarial stance. Bierbaum referred to "applied lyrics" which, like applied art, would appeal to the heterogeneity and short attention spans of the urban audiences.

Wolzogen acted as conférencier, presenting recitations of poetry as well as erotic songs, literary parody, pantomime, one-act plays, and Bierbaum's rousing round-dance, "The Merry Husband," with music by Oscar Straus, which became the Überbrettl's most famous number:

Ring around the rose garland,
I'm dancing with my wife:
We dance around the rosebush,
Klingklangglorybush;
I spin like a top through life.

It was all very much to the *Jugendstil* taste, and became so popular it haunted its author to his death.

The writers for the Überbrettl included the novelist of the supernatural Hanns Heinz Ewers, the journalist Max Hirschfeld (b.1860) and the poet Christian Morgenstern (1871-1914), whose nonsense verse and attacks on literary convention received their first real audience there. A follower of Nietzsche and Rudolph Steiner, he injected his burlesque with metaphysical implications, taking conventional phrases literally and creating new entities by means of verbal analogues. His *Gallows Songs* were first heard at the Motley Theatre, since they were too novel to be published.

As time went on, the Motley Theatre grew too popular to suit Wolzogen's exclusive tastes. In 1902, after he bowed out, it became an operetta theatre with an Überbrettl department and folded the following year.

Manifesto for a Cabaret Theatre
(from *Stilpe*)

1897

by

Otto Julius Bierbaum

[Stilpe's plans for the Momus Theatre:] ''Yes, yes: all art and all life, to be reborn, by way of the music hall! . . . We'll drag everything into our net: painting, versifying, singing, everything that has beauty and the joy of life in it. What is art nowadays? A miniscule, shimmering spider web in a cranny of life. We will spread it as a golden net over all the people, all life. All those who have hitherto avoided the theatre as anxiously as they do the church will come to us. And even though they come only for a bit of entertainment, we'll show them what they've been missing: the true gaiety that enlightens life, the art of dance in words, sounds, colors, contours, gestures. Naked joy in loveliness; wit that takes the world by the ear; fantasy that juggles with the stars and rope-dances on the whiskers of the Cosmos: the philosophy of harmonious laughter; the hurray of a soul in torment . . . ah, we shall work in life itself as the troubadours did! We shall bring a new civilization dancing into the world! We will give birth to the Superman in our halls! We will stand this silly world on its head; crown indecency as the only decency; once more raise nudity in all its beauty on high before all the people . . . Ah, the things we'll make the stolid burghers of Germania do, when once we inject them with this spirit . . .

''Look at the theatres! Empty! Look at the Wintergarten Palace of Variety! Full. One dying; the other flourishing . . . The day of the theatre is over . . . Just as the theatre, once an annex of the church, got loose and found a form suitable to its era, so the art of today must emancipate itself from the theatre and choose the form determined by the taste of our times: the form of the music hall! Both are ripe for decline: the theatre because it is too clumsy, too ponderous, too static for the hard-drinking appetite of our latter-day art-lovers; and the present-day music hall, because it does not know how to express all the neurotic desires and emotions of our times artistically. Let us found a music hall based on art in the widest meaning of the term . . .

"The object of our Hall is to do away with the last vestiges of interest in all this literature of yours. We want to make the people of Berlin truly aesthetic. There are still people who read books. That's got to stop. There's more lyricism in the lace panties of my soubrettes than in all your published works; and when the time comes when I can let them dance without any panties at all, even you will realize that the only verses that ever need to be written are those sung on our stage. Beautiful costumes, beautiful arms, bosoms, legs, gestures—that's what counts. Develop dances for me; devise pantomimes; solve for me the problem of emancipation from tights —that's what I need. And if you absolutely have to write verses, don't forget they must be sung by beautiful girls whose corsets embrace more than the void . . ."

House Rules for the Motley Theatre
(Hausordnung für das Buntes Theater)
1901
by
Ernst von Wolzogen

1. The honorable performers are required, without exception, to appear in the theatre by 7 o'clock p.m. and to go over the program with the stage managers.

2. Those performers who are not involved in the evening's program are required to specify where they may be found during the performance.

3. The performers must keep strictly to the program, and to the turns assigned to them as well. Reasonable requests to alter the prescribed turns are to be addressed well in advance to the manager, or to his deputies, in musical matters to the chief conductor, or to his deputies.

4. The stage manager is to attend to the strict observance of the program and to report any offense against it.

5. Every performer has approximately ten minutes before the beginning of his turn to prepare for his entrance. The stage manager is to call the performers to the stage punctually by means of bells and in cases where they are not ready in time for their entrance, to send out the succeeding performer in the program, the omitted turn to be dropped and the relevant performer to be slated for a fine by the stage manager.

6. To prevent disturbances and noise, the performers are requested to refrain backstage from any loud talk, unnecessary movement to and fro, door-slamming, etc., and to remain after the conclu-

sion of their turn as much as possible in the dressing rooms or green rooms.

7. Gentlemen are not allowed to enter ladies' dressing rooms nor are ladies allowed to enter gentlemen's dressing rooms. Visitors, even family members, may not be received either in the dressing rooms or on stage.

8. Performers not taking part may enter the auditorium, so long as they avoid any disturbing movement in and out as well as any behavior that draws attention to themselves.

Egon and Emilia

(Egon und Emilie)

Not a Domestic Tragedy

c. 1901

by

Christian Morgenstern

(*The stage represents a cozy living room. In the left corner a chimney nook with a settle. Center a round table. Windows, doors.*)

EMILIA: (*Pulling Egon into the room by his hand.*) In here! That's right, in here, my darling Egon! Oh how happy I am, how happy your Emilia is! (*She gazes at Egon with eyes aglitter.*) But you say nothing at all—

EGON: (*Sits on the sofa and holds his peace.*)

EMILIA: Have you no word for our happiness? But surely—(*She falters.*)

EGON: (*Is silent.*)

EMILIA: (*On the settle.*) I should have guessed it! I should have foreseen it! I'm a wretched creature! I'm a fool! But my God, all may not yet be lost—am I right, Egon (*she leaps up, in intense anguish*), am I right, Egon?

EGON: (*Is silent.*)

EMILIA: Oh, I implore you! Speak but a word, just one single little word!

EGON: (*Is silent.*)

EMILIA: (*At the round table.*) Oh, for heaven's sake—is it so impossible, this thing I ask for, no beg for, plead for! I do not want your forgiveness or your understanding, no, not for a long while yet, we still have a good five acts for that, but let me have some point of contact, don't deny me some cue—

EGON: (*Is silent.*)

EMILIA: (*Out the window.*) Egon! Egon!!—Egon!!!

EGON: (*Is silent.*)

EMILIA: (*To him.*) Are you aware, shameless creature, that this is the death of me? That now I cannot develop into a character—all on account of your infamous silence? That I must now leave this stage, exit into the nameless void, without ever having acted or lived? (*She pulls out her watch and waits for a full minute.*) No answer, no inarticulate sound, not even a glance! Stone, stone, ice. Cruel wretch, you who have murdered my role, unnatural man, you who have strangled a domestic tragedy in its diapers . . . He is dumb, he sits there dumb, I go. Now, curtain, ring down once more, though you have scarcely been up; dear people, return home. You saw, I did what I could. All in vain. This brute wants no tragedy, he wants his peace and quiet. Farewell. (*Exits.*)

EGON: (*Rises.*) Quite right; I want my peace and quiet, I want no domestic tragedy. For your sake, dear spectator, am I to be at the mercy of this Niagara Falls of a woman? To be implicated with her in endless rigmarole before your lovely eyes? I think not. Now go home and consider that today for the first time in your life you have seen a truly rational man on stage, a man who not only pays lip service to the adage "Speech is silver, silence is golden," but fearlessly lives by it. Farewell. (*Exits.*)

Yes, Mama!

(*Ja, Mama!*)

1902

by

Max Hirschfeld

(*Living room. Alice enters, uneasy and preoccupied. Picks up a big doll . . . and tosses it disdainfully over her shoulder. She hears her Mother enter . . .*)

MOTHER: Come here, Alice! . . . You are eighteen years old, it is high time to stop playing with dolls once and for all, and a young girl must have more serious interests . . . Have you ever considered what you want to be in the future?

ALICE: (*Earnestly.*) Yes, Mama!

MOTHER: I'm glad of that . . . Vanity in moderation is the mother of all feminine virtues. . . . Have you ever considered that you might be married soon?

ALICE: (*Smiling in embarrassment.*) Yes, Mama!

MOTHER: Very good . . . Nowadays mothers no longer go husband hunting for their daughters—at least only in very rare cases—nowadays the daughters themselves have to . . . take a brisk hand in it, if something comes your way—something acceptable of course. I have . . . had a look around myself—unfortunately I haven't found anything passable . . . Do you recall Herr von Eichstädt?

ALICE: (*Wincing.*) Yes, Mama!

MOTHER: All right then. Martin von Eichstädt is a son-in-law after my own heart, a decent young man with good manners and a comfortable position in life . . . But Alice, you smile so strangely, have you already exchanged views with Herr von Eichstädt on this matter?

ALICE: (*Snivelling.*) Yes, Mama!

MOTHER: Don't look down at the floor, child, that's false modesty. This sort of skirmishing does more than enhance one's charms . . . For example, he will hold your hand on the sly and squeeze it. Decency demands that you pull it away, at least the first time . . . Or did you, you silly little goose, already exchange the aforementioned hand-squeezes with Herr von Eichstädt?

ALICE: (*With sudden resolution.*) Yes, Mama!

MOTHER: . . . Alice, you're confusing me—perhaps in a few weeks I may ask: has he kissed you?

ALICE: (*Sitting up straight, calmly.*) Yes, Mama!

MOTHER: . . . Do you mean to tell me . . . that he . . . that the two of you kissed?

ALICE: (*Weeping.*) Yes, Mama!

MOTHER: I am speechless. Words literally fail me. Well, never mind . . . (*The maid brings in a letter, the Mother reads it in surprise.*) Just imagine, Alice, what I have here. Martin von Eichstädt is making a proposal. He has just asked for your hand.

ALICE: (*Throwing herself impetuously on her Mother's bosom.*) Oh God, Mama, it was—high time!

NEARLY FORTY-FIVE CABARETS OPENED IN BERLIN BETWEEN 1901 and 1905, although most of them leaned more towards vaudeville than *cabaret artistique*. Morgenstern could be said to be the inspiration of the best of these, the *Schall und Rauch*, because it was conceived as a benefit performance to subsidize his stay in a Swiss tuberculosis sanitarium.

Max Reinhardt (1873-1943) was an actor at the Deutsches Theater when, with his colleagues the actor Friedrich Kayssler and the director Martin Zickel, he formed the artist's club *Die Brille* (The Eyeglasses) in 1894. In 1898/99 the group presented satiric scenes and improvised one-acts once a week, and when they staged the Morgenstern benefit on January 23, 1901, their success inspired them to establish a literary cabaret. The title referred to a line from Goethe, ''A name is but a little bit of noise and a puff of smoke (*Schall und Rauch*).'' They set up in the Arnim Hotel on Unter den Linden, where they presented musical and theatrical parodies for a histrionic in-crowd. Their earliest success was Schiller's *Don Carlos* staged four different ways: as a fit-up melodrama performed by an itinerant troupe of hams, as a naturalistic play of slum life by Hauptmann, as a symbolist mystery by Maeterlinck, and as a Überbrettl sketch. They also devised the popular duo Serenissimus and Kindermann, a dim-witted German princeling and his well-meaning chancellor, a barely veiled attack on the philistinism of Wilhelm II.

Gradually, as the audience became more mixed, the in-jokes began to be replaced by one-act plays, the cabaret atmosphere changed to a kind of chamber theatre, and in 1903 the Schall und Rauch was renamed the Little Theatre, where Reinhardt earned fame as a director with his productions of *Salome, Elektra,* and *The Lower Depths.*

A Course in Stage Directing
(Das Regie-Kollegium)
A Mood Piece Based on a Stage Rehearsal
1901
by
Max Reinhardt

MAIN CHARACTERS:
The Prompter
The Manager
The Director
The Actor
The Stage Manager

INCIDENTAL CHARACTER:
The Author

PLACE: A Stage

TIME: Morning

NOTES FOR STAGING

A stage seen from behind during a rehearsal. Therefore only the back of the wing-pieces are visible. The prompter's box is turned to the audience. The curtain is located somewhere in the middle distance of the stage. It is closed or let down and similarly displays only its reverse side. Before the curtain, left of the prompter's box, three chairs and a director's desk are set and at right stands a table. (If possible also footlights turned to the audience.) The rest of the stage is assumed to be in the audience and those who play the Director, the Manager, and the Author speak into the audience when they address the Actor. The actual rehearsal will also be assumed to take place over the heads of the audience.

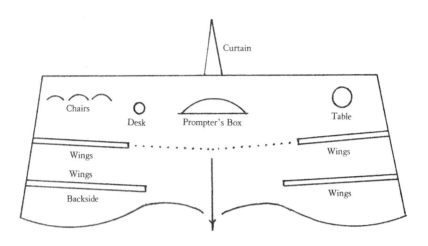

When the curtain rises, the stage remains empty for a moment, then:

AUTHOR: (*Enters left in haste, looks around in haste. He is wearing an overcoat, holds his hat in his hand and his play under his arm. A fair-haired young man in up-to-date clothing, timid and nervous.*) Anybody here? (*He looks at his watch as he shakes his head and speaks out.*) Ah, please, sir, ah, please! (*Louder.*) Is there anybody here? . . . What? . . . Oh? . . . Aha . . . Yes, but the rehearsal is set for 10 o'clock and now . . . well, all right. (*Walks up and down restlessly, stares into space, makes theatrical gestures, looks for different things in his script and sits down for a moment.*) There's a chill here, a draft, and even if there weren't I'm already (*leaps up again to see if anyone's coming, stands in place, gets impatient, asks again:*) Ah, please! You!—Ah, might I ask if you'd be so kind, it's now almost a quarter to eleven, would you mind looking in the office . . . What's that? . . . What? . . . How do you mean? . . . All right, but (*looks at his watch*), in that case we won't be ready—

DIRECTOR: (*Enters left, dictatorial, unmannerly, a martinet, robust, dryly impassive, hat and cape.*) Mornin', mornin', my boy. Ah, our author! Howarya? Filthy weather, right? To hell with it. This damned rehearsal nonsense. (*Rubs his hands together.*)

AUTHOR: (*Friendly and self-conscious.*) Ah, yes, yes of course, yes, yes it's rather cool in here too, I think there's a draft somewhere, and even if there weren't I haven't been up to snuff ever since rehearsals began. And this bad weather, do you think it will have an effect on the attendance? Do you?

DIRECTOR: Ah, rubbish, poppycock! Psst, Mostrich!

STAGE MANAGER: (*From left, helps him off with his cape.*) Mornin', mornin' Herr Directah.

DIRECTOR: Mornin'. Everything all right? Eh?

STAGE MANAGER: Yessir, yessir. (*Exits left with the cape and hat.*)

DIRECTOR: (*Rubs his hands together, whistles, blows his nose.*)

AUTHOR: Ah, Herr Chief Director, I'd like—

DIRECTOR: (*Sharply.*) What? (*Unwraps a sandwich, starts to eat, listens with one ear.*)

AUTHOR: (*Tries to make a joke out of it.*) Bon appetit.

DIRECTOR: (*Curtly.*) Thanks.

AUTHOR: (*Apprehensively.*) Ah, Herr Chief Director, I've taken the liberty—at the last rehearsal of my play there were all sorts of things—that's not what I'm here for—now I've carefully noted them down—

DIRECTOR: (*Listens impassively while eating.*)

AUTHOR: So first I mean, might, I think, Herr Schmalzer this—

DIRECTOR: (*Roaring out.*) Hey, Fuchsdorf! Confound it! Where's he put that chair again? I expressly arranged things just yesterday so that—what? . . . Rubbish! It should be on the right, muttonhead, write it down behind your ears, or next time I'll get nasty. The things that go on around here are unbelievable.

AUTHOR: (*Tries to continue his speech.*) Yes, so I was thinking Herr Schmalzer should really play these passages on which I place the greatest value with more—

DIRECTOR: (*Shouts.*) Mostrich, Mostrich! (*Screams.*) Mostrich! Confound it, where's the fellow hiding?

STAGE MANAGER: (*From left.*) Yes, Herr Directah?

DIRECTOR: Where were you hiding, damn it? A man can scream his lungs out! I'll have to get nasty.

STAGE MANAGER: Excuse me, Herr Schmalzer isn't here yet, I had to see about it.

DIRECTOR: Naturally, probably still in bed. Lazy beast! Unbelievable these late-comers, they'll turn me nasty. Mostrich, go tell Fräulein Sturzbach . . . (*Pulls Mostrich to one side and asks a*

question, Mostrich answers, nothing but muttering and laughter can be heard for a while.)
AUTHOR: (*Stands there at a loss.*)
DIRECTOR: (*Aloud again.*) All right now, don't let it happen again, there should be none of that here, this is no small-time touring company, tell 'em that if you please.
STAGE MANAGER: (*With a grin.*) Yessir, Herr Directah. (*Exits.*)
DIRECTOR: (*Is still smiling in remembrance of the conversation he just had, folds up the sandwich paper and sticks it in his pocket.*)
AUTHOR: (*Tries another assault.*) Um, excuse me, I mean, just here towards the end of Act Two, Herr Schmalzer must bring more sunshine into the scene, the words must be filled with more light, I conceived of it as something liberating. (*The Director goes past the Author to the other side, the Author follows him.*) This is precisely one of the brightest points in my play, there might even be some humor maybe—naturally not coarse comedy, but a fine line between tragedy and comedy might be drawn through these words, I mean that—(*He sees that the Director has not listened for a moment.*)
DIRECTOR: (*Smiles at the arriving actors who are assumed to be in the auditorium, wags a finger at them and mumbles to himself.*) Damned bitch! Greetings, salutations! Sure, of course, etc.
AUTHOR: (*Greets them mechanically at first. Then following up:*) Herr Director.
DIRECTOR: (*Irritated.*) What is it? What is it? What is it?
AUTHOR: (*Bewildered.*) I mean, I thought, I believed Herr Schmalzer could draw a fine line through—maybe more sunshine—naturally, I know. (*Fades out.*)
DIRECTOR: (*Looks at him dully.*) Well then, what about it? What about it? What about it? Just what do you want, huh?
AUTHOR: I only mean that I took the liberty—I was thinking that the whole thing could—in other words, I mean, Herr Schmalzer in particular could perhaps bring out the words (*leafs through his script*) in the second act somewhat more aromatically and brightly, sunbeams should flit over these passages, a lightly sparkling but still melancholy humor should flicker in them.
DIRECTOR: Sure, sure, of course! We know that anyway, we all know that, we're doing it already, just take it easy, it'll all be there. Herr Schmalzer will do it.
AUTHOR: Yes, but maybe it could be pointed out to him.

DIRECTOR: (*Yawns.*) Yes, by the way we have to make a couple of cuts. The thing's much too long as it is. Nobody'll sit through it.

AUTHOR: (*Taken aback.*) You think so? But there's already been so many cuts, there's hardly anything left but the skeleton, it's turning into another play entirely.

DIRECTOR: Sure, sure, but that's the main thing, you should be glad, that's what it's all about. Just leave it to me, please. (*They sit down. The Director takes out a script, reads it, yawning constantly and with a thick pencil makes rapid cuts, shearing away whole pages.*)

AUTHOR: (*Looks on sorrowfully and aggrieved, every cut is a dagger-thrust to him, he winces, wants to intervene, but lets himself be frightened off by the Director's nonchalantly violent manner.*)

DIRECTOR: (*Leafing through further on, murmuring.*) There! That stuff's all pointless, just holds things up unnecessarily. (*Mute business.*)

AUTHOR: (*Desperately.*) No, no, Herr Chief Director, that simply won't do, those are exactly the sunny passages I had promised myself would have such a beautiful effect, couldn't we—(*Tries to intervene.*)

DIRECTOR: (*Makes no answer, calmly keeps on cutting.*)

AUTHOR: (*Sweating by now.*) But, Herr Director, this is quite impossible! You are butchering my play!

DIRECTOR: (*Silently keeps cutting and yawning.*)

AUTHOR: (*Leaping up in the most intense grief.*) No, this is unacceptable! This is quite unacceptable! This is absolutely unacceptable! I shall have to withdraw my play!

DIRECTOR: (*Mutters something, keeps cutting.*)

(*Meanwhile the Prompter has been seen to enter his box, peacefully eats an apple and greets the actors.*)

STAGE MANAGER: (*Appears with the bell.*)

DIRECTOR: (*Has now cut the last page.*) There!—Mostrich, everybody here? Then let's get on with it! Prompter here? Huh?

PROMPTER: (*From the box.*) Here, Herr Chief Director, good morning.

DIRECTOR: Mornin'. (*Flings him the cut script.*) Come on then, let's get on with it! (*Yawns.*)

AUTHOR: (*Suffering.*) Oh please, please, just a minute, I just have to—I'll be right back. (*Rushes out.*)

DIRECTOR: Jesus Christ, what's wrong with him? (*Looks in his direction.*) Ah, that's it! (*Mutters.*) He could have gone earlier. (*Pause.*) Unbelievable!

STAGE MANAGER: (*Smirks.*)

AUTHOR: (*Comes back, buttoning up his coat, suffering and resigned.*)

DIRECTOR: (*Brusquely, impatiently.*) Now let's get on with it! Come on! Mood! Mood! Tempo, tempo! Keep it moving briskly, don't camp on it. All right: curtain!

STAGE MANAGER: (*Buzzes the bell twice.*)

PROMPTER: (*Prompts. It is noticeable that for one actor he over-exerts himself and repeats lines loudly, while for others he merely gives hints and whispers. Long pause. Pantomime.*)

DIRECTOR: (*Listens, bored, to part of it, pulls out a hand-mirror, brushes his hair and beard.*)

AUTHOR: (*Would like to break in, sits very restlessly, speaks along with all the lines, often his face is distorted in intense agony, he winces. Finally he can't stand it anymore and whispers in excitement to the Director.*)

DIRECTOR: (*First mutters something, then:*) Confound it, Herr Schmalzer, didn't you get a good night's sleep? What were you doing *last night* then? Sleep *at home* and *here* show a little passion! Don't be so wishy-washy, so namby-pamby, it'll drive me to drink. I've told you a good thousand times, this stuff is thin enough without that—What?—Don't talk nonsense! *Naturally* that's what it's meant to be! It's as clear as mud.

AUTHOR: (*Rises faint-hearted.*) Yes, Herr Schmalzer, I mean, I conceived of this moment as a very particular mood—we still have to find the exact technique to express it, it should be like the first faint pale sunbeams after a violent storm—a lightly awakening but cheerful vigor must patter down through the words and I was thinking—

MANAGER: (*Enters in an overcoat and a broad-brimmed hat, hands in his pockets. Corpulent. Pince-nez on his nose. His face always bears a highly dissatisfied expression which never brightens up. He speaks very slowly and whiningly.*)

DIRECTOR: (*Jumps up.*) Morning, Herr Manager.

MANAGER: (*With closed mouth.*) Mm. (*Answers the greetings of the Author and the Actors the same way. Sits down, keeping his hat on.*)

AUTHOR: (*Greeting him, wants to say more.*) So I was thinking—

DIRECTOR: (*Now very eager.*) Let's get on with it! Come on! We've got to keep moving!

AUTHOR: But I really would like—a bit more sunshine—

DIRECTOR: (*Cutting him off.*) Yes, yes, fine, fine, that'll all get done! Let's go!

PROMPTER: (*During the previous speeches has serenely eaten his apple again, looks round and then goes on prompting as before. Pause. Pantomime. Prompts as before. Pantomime.*)

MANAGER: (*Sits in discontent, from time to time utters a disapproving grunt.*)

DIRECTOR: (*Observes the Manager and reacts to his utterances by tearing his hair, stamping his feet, etc.*)

AUTHOR: (*Sits as in a dentist's chair, groans, distorts his face in agony, keeps wanting to break in, doesn't dare to—finally withdraws hurriedly.*)

MANAGER: (*In reaction to that questions with a few quiet grunts.*)

DIRECTOR: (*Disdainfully whispers the answer to him.*)

MANAGER: Hmhm—Already?

AUTHOR: (*Comes back. Whispers to the Director from time to time.*)

DIRECTOR: (*Does not react.*)

MANAGER: (*Niggling.*) But, Herr Schmalzer, you don't know your lines again! No—I can hear it—You constantly stutter! The character is not a stutterer. The audience will notice. (*The Actor is assumed to reply.*)

PROMPTER: Me?—Excuse me please, Herr Schmalzer. I have been putting myself out for you quite a bit!—I prompt loud enough as it happens!—Well, that's not so!

DIRECTOR: (*Roars.*) You don't know a word of it! You never stop ad-libbing! We won't put up with it—we've had enough of it—that's why this man is here! (*Indicates the Author.*) We're fed up with this!—What? (*Sharply.*) How's that? Yes, yes, we know—a poor excuse!—You'd do better to learn your lines, instead of chasing skirts all day long. Let's get on with it! Let's go! (*Claps his hands. Pause. Pantomime.*)

MANAGER: (*To the Prompter.*) Please, Herr Nightly—that is a pause! Don't keep giving prompts in the pauses! The pauses are the best things in this play! (*The Director laughs in assent.*)

AUTHOR: (*Whispers something else to the Director.*)

DIRECTOR: (*Wearily.*) The author wants more sunshine, Herr Schmalzer! More sunshine! So give him sunshine already!

MANAGER: Yes, why don't you provide more sunshine? What do you get your salary for? Speak a little more sunnily. The audience always enjoys sunshine on the stage. What?—But it's ever so simple! Like this . . . (*He speaks a line, which the Prompter gives him, without much expression.*) Like that!—It's really not a great deal to ask. Absurdly simple . . .

DIRECTOR: Please, don't laugh Herr Schmalzer! It violates the house rules.

MANAGER: (*Annoyed.*) Mostrich, put down Herr Schmalzer for a fine.

DIRECTOR: Let's go, let's get on with it. (*Pause. Pantomime. The Author goes outside.*)

MANAGER: What did you say? How does the speech go? Herr Nightly, please . . .

PROMPTER: (*Reads a speech meekly.*)

MANAGER: Aha! I didn't understand a word of it. (*To the Director.*) Did you understand any of it?

DIRECTOR: (*Phlegmatically.*) Not a syllable.

MANAGER: (*Plaintively.*) Well, that's why people stop going to the theatre! Why should they pay when they can't understand?! They might just as well go to the waxworks. What?—Oh so! They're simply destroying my theatre!

DIRECTOR: All right, Herr Schmalzer, louder! Damn it, are you tongue-tied today? An actor should be able to talk!—

MANAGER: Oh, Herr Nightly, please don't shout like that. You musn't prompt so loudly.—The audience doesn't want to hear the play twice. Once is quite enough . . .

DIRECTOR: (*Laughs loudly.*) Let's get on with it! (*Pause. Pantomime.*)

MANAGER: (*Whispers something to the Director.*)

DIRECTOR: Stop, stop! (*Claps his hands.*) Stop! That just won't do, Herr Schmalzer! It won't do! That's the way they act in Lower Slobbovia—I don't follow you! —But it's so simple! Pay attention! (*Acts it out, shouts.*) You take the letter nice and calmly, go to the table nice and calmly, and put the letter on the table nice and calmly. (*Bangs furiously on the table.*)

AUTHOR: (*Wants to say something.*) Ah, I'd like, I mean that . . .

maybe a little more sunshine—

DIRECTOR: (*Cutting him off.*) Yes, yes, I've already shown him how to do that! Therefore the matter is closed.—Let's gooooo.—

MANAGER: (*Wriggling.*) No, no, Herr Schmalzer! You're falling asleep! More temperament—(*showing him*) more passion! (*Kicks out his foot.*) Look—like this! The audience wants passion! Be passionate, Herr Schmalzer . . .

AUTHOR: (*Whispers something to the Director.*) Excuse me!

DIRECTOR: Ssst! Stop, stop, stop, stop! Stop your talent for a second, Herr Schmalzer! The author wants to speak to you himself. (*Resigned.*) Please go ahead for chrissake! (*He closes his eyes.*)

AUTHOR: Forgive me for interrupting you, Herr Schmalzer. But I believe you've misunderstood the situation. If perhaps you were to put less emphasis on realism and more on that light, sunny mood—

MANAGER: But of course, it stands to reason! Mood! Mood is the most important thing! Mood is up-to-date. Nowadays people demand mood. (*Whining.*) Give us some mood, Schmalzer.

DIRECTOR: Ye Gods and little fishes, are you totally godforsaken? Schmalzer! (*Roars like one possessed.*) You must supply mood! Mood, mood!! Damn it! Mood! (*Brief pause.*)

MANAGER: Please, Schmalzer, for heaven's sake! Be more elegant. You're playing a lover. Lovers move quite differently. You ought to know that. They undulate like an old earthworm. More refined, more elegant, Schmalzer! Look, like this. (*He flings back his overcoat and takes a few would-be elegant, comically wobbling steps.*) Something like that. (*To the Author.*) Wasn't that the way you conceived the role?

AUTHOR: (*Cautiously.*) Yes, perhaps even a bit *more* elegant and then—after all that's an external. But the essence of the thing must become better molded. It is your task, Herr Schmalzer, to lay bare the nervous system of the work. Everything is still too blurry, too cliché. If you could perhaps apply more vivid, sunny, sensual colors.

MANAGER: Naturally! It stands to reason! More sensual, much more sensual! I've always told you, a lover should be sensual beyond anything else. So be sensual, Schmalzer. A person can ask that of you surely. It's frightfully easy.

AUTHOR: Ah, if I might take the liberty, a few words—

DIRECTOR: Be my guest. (*Leans back with a sigh.*)

AUTHOR: (*Faltering, groping for the words.*) So, Herr Schmalzer, if I might tell you something—I mean, if we could perhaps work this out: it has to be a ganglion of sensations.

DIRECTOR: (*Quietly.*) Oh my sainted aunt!

AUTHOR: —You might perhaps call it a harmony. The keynote is of course paroxysm and inner turmoil, but the inner turmoil of someone convalescing—an inner turmoil which is part of the healing process. A healing inner turmoil, a total inner turmoil—and along with it sunshine, a great deal of sunshine, the subdued, beaming sunshine of spring.—What?—What do you mean?—Yes, but why couldn't you do that?—What?—But I've just laid it out for you so clearly. There's nothing more to be said.—What do you mean?—Please, please! (*Offended; to the others.*) Well, if Herr Schmalzer is incapable of doing this, then I'm very sorry. Please excuse me! Excuse me! In that case I must *unfortunately* insist that you cooperate with my intentions. After all I am the one who wrote the play. I must therefore have given it a great deal of thought—What do you mean, Herr Schmalzer? —You doubt that?—Very well, gentlemen, Herr Schmalzer chooses to have his joke. What do you say to that. (*Silence.*) Very well, gentlemen, then there is no point to any of this—absolutely no point—and I am superfluous here?—(*A dull, oppressive pause.*) Indeed! Well, then I can go, then I shall go, yes, well then, I'm going. Adieu, gentlemen. I'm going. (*He sits down, very upset. Stubborn silence.*) Well? Well? In that case I shall withdraw my play!—All right, I am withdrawing my play.

MANAGER: (*Impassive.*) Nothing but empty promises.

AUTHOR: Excuse me, I shall reserve the right to withdraw my play!

DIRECTOR: But, gentlemen, why should we get hung up on this *theoretical* question. There's absolutely *no practical* basis to it. Please, Herr Schmalzer, come over here! There's no point in going on with the rehearsal today! Once Herr Schmalzer knows his lines, he'll give you so much sunshine you'll get sunstroke. (*The three worthies murmur excitedly with each other.*)

ACTOR: (*A fat, phlegmatic type appears, totally fagged out, bathed in sweat, his face glowing with grease, and waits.*)

MANAGER: (*Impressively.*) Ah, Herr Schmalzer, please. (*Draws him aside.*) You're too flat, Herr Schmalzer. You must make more concessions to the audience. Don't let yourself be distracted by what the others say. You're too hard, it's indigestible, the audience wants mellowness. So be elegant, be moody, be passionate, Schmalzer, be sensual and above all be *mellow*, Schmalzer! (*Goes to the Author and calms him down.*)

DIRECTOR: (*Affably.*) Schmalzer, don't get snowed under by all this guff! They're just dolts! It's all very good, only you're *too* mellow, much too mellow, Schmalzer! That's the one fault. Stronger, harder, *louder, much louder!* (*Claps him on the shoulder. Benevolently.*) Well, it'll get there! Just be louder!

AUTHOR: (*Nervously, timidly.*) Dear Herr Schmalzer, you see, I don't mean to keep at you all the time, but you are *much too loud*, I've conceived of this as much more subdued, more quiet and more refined! You see (*takes the script*) I have conceived that there must be more sunshine here—

ACTOR: (*Grins broadly.*)

AUTHOR: (*Silently takes his hat and cloak, greatly upset; goes to the Manager.*) Very well, dear Herr Manager, when an author's words evoke nothing but mirth in your institution, when your actors are incapable of creating even a little bit of sunshine, then I give it up! I withdraw my play, I shall have it published, I shall never again, never again set foot on this stage. Please do not try to hold me back! Never again! (*Rushes out.*)

MANAGER: (*Furiously to the Director.*) Yes, dear Herr Director. You are destroying my theatre! There's no way to stop it. Yes, yes, when you can't stage even so weak a play as this. This is really unbelievable; any hack touring director could produce a little sunshine; there's some in every play. Oh please, leave me in peace, it's over, it's over, it's over! (*He exits. Pause. For a while an outburst of bad language can be heard backstage.*)

DIRECTOR: (*Roaring wildly at the Actor.*) Stop grinning, Schmalzhead! You know I've seen plenty of faces in my time, but I've never come across a countenance as attractive as yours. I'll have to gird my damn loins to resist such charms. (*Gesticulation.*) You lack the most elementary understanding. Every babe in arms knows what sunshine is, and you stand there like, like—Herr Schmalzer up against a road block! Once, just once I wish you lots of sunshine, Herr Schmalzer. Maybe then you'll melt away! That would be a blessing. (*Exits.*)

ACTOR: (*Stops grinning and suddenly says rabidly to the Prompter.*) You night owl you! Couldn't you prompt a little louder?

Why are you making a mystery out of this piece of crap? You could safely trust me with this rubbish. You hiss like an old garter snake! How am I supposed to create sunshine when I always have to have such an old heap of night soil before my eyes. (*Exits.*)

PROMPTER: (*Repeating sorrowfully.*) Night soil! (*He swallows the insult, slams the script shut, and disappears.*)

STAGE MANAGER: (*Enters and moves the table.*)

AUTHOR: (*Appears and asks hastily.*) Herr Stage Manager, what time tomorrow is the rehearsal?

STAGE MANAGER: The rehearsal? Ten o'clock.

THE CURTAIN FALLS

ONE OF THE ACTORS FROM THE DEUTSCHES THEATER WHO AP-
peared at *Schall und Rauch* was the Viennese Rudolf Bernauer
(1880-1953). With his colleague Carl Meinhard, he opened a new
Berlin literary cabaret *Die Böse Buben* (The Bad Boys or Naughty
Boys). The first performance was given on 16 November 1901 at
the Künstlerhaus in Bellevuestrasse. The Bad Boys performed only
occasionally for an invited audience, and thus managed to last until
1905.

The Bad Boys satirized other cabarets' offerings, particularly the
Überbrettl's "Merry Husband," and presented social commen-
tary in song, as in "The Underprivileged" (*Die Minderwertigen*)
which kidded the psychiatric exoneration of criminals. But, as with
Reinhardt, their specialty was dramatic parody, the most famous being the ending of Ibsen's *A Doll's House* as rewritten by Wedekind,
Maeterlinck, and the Kaiser's favorite playwright, the bombastic
and chauvinistic Joseph Lauff. The audience remembered that when
Ibsen's play had first been produced in Germany in 1880, the
Munich theatre management had insisted on a happy ending, and
they tumultuously acclaimed Bernauer's travesty.

An Evening at the Bad Boys' Cabaret
(from *Das Theater meines Lebens*)

1951

by

Rudolf Bernauer

The curtains parted. The four "Bad Boys," Carlchen Meinhard, Rudelchen Bernauer, Paulchen Schweiger, and Leo Wulff came before the footlights in short pants and Eton collars. In doggerel verse, they introduced themselves and Leo Fall who was pounding the piano. Then a quarrel broke out as to who would speak the prologue. Since none of them had the guts to do it, like children they had a counting-out game. The counter-outers recited in sing-song all the super gaffs in Berlin:

> Super-gaff—Secession,
> Wolzogehn and Liliencron,
> Flat-irons—Muse's Stall,
> Seventh Heaven—Rauch und Schall,
> High Arts and Rhapsody,
> Trianon—Charivari,
> So on, so forth, on and up
> Down to Trudie's Mongrel's Pup!
> Unbound Pages—Pegasus,
> The Bad Boys put an end to this.

Those who were "counted out" disappeared backstage, and at the end only "the host" Leo Wulff was left over; he bowed stiffly, started to stutter and finally instead of a prologue pronounced a necrologue. Then he disappeared too. People laughed . . . Then suddenly an elegant gentleman stood up in the stalls. He was holding a program, which he leafed through superciliously. He disclosed to the audience that the "Boys" had asked him to undertake the job of master of ceremonies today, because the performer assigned to that task had begged off. He was ready to do so for courtesy's sake, although he considered any introduction to be wholly superfluous. It's all there in the program, and he really doesn't care for these pitchman's announcements of which artistes are to appear. Whether Fräulein X is really incomparable or Herr Y is actually that remarkable should be left to the audience to decide . . . And now, shaking his head, he read from the list the title of the next number: "The Merry Husband," the most frequently performed item at the Super-gaff. The gentleman pulled a very sour face. He gave his opinion it was not worth staying up all night just to hear this duet. If the Boys haven't anything better to offer, he won't grow gray here. Now Fall began his introduction on the piano. The curtain rose on a couple in Biedermeier costume, accompanied by "Ring around the rosy, I'm dancing with my wife." But right after the first bar the gentleman crossly interrupted the singing and explained that on the audience's behalf he magnanimously dispensed with this duet. These interpolations seemed so genuine that this "refined gathering" never suspected that they were a rehearsed performance. The role was taken by the actor Ivald. Although familiar to many, he was not suspected in the least, even though other theatre people were among the spectators . . . There were calls of "Sit down!," "Humbug" or "Next Act." Other spectators insisted that the disconcerted couple on stage be allowed to go on singing. But most protested, and the pair disappeared from the stage.

Now Leo Fall played a short comic variation, whose finale, however, obviously turned into the introduction to "The Merry Husband." The curtain was rapidly rung up, and Paul Schweiger appeared in a startlingly real make-up as the famous painter Professor Lenbach, leading by the hand the world-renowned dancer Saharet, whom everyone knew either from seeing her in the theatre "or from the illustrated papers." Just at that time Lenbach had painted Saharet, and not only was the picture considered one of his most interesting, but everyone whispered about certain relations between painter and model. To the Straus tune and in words adapted from Bierbaum they began to sing about their merry friendship . . . The make-ups were so pointedly caricatured and yet so lifelike, that each one was immediately greeted with applause. The success was all the greater, since many people really thought at first a riot would break out in the theatre.

A Doll's House
(Nora)
Last Act, Last Scene
Adapted by Frank Wedekind, Maurice
Maeterlinck, and Joseph Lauff
1903
by
Rudolf Bernauer

(*The last scene of the original* A Doll's House *begins with the lines:*)

HELMER: What is this? Aren't you going to bed? You've changed your clothes?

NORA: (*In her everyday clothes.*) Yes, Torvald, I have changed my clothes.

HELMER: But what for? Now? So late?

NORA: I will not sleep tonight.

HELMER: But, Nora dear—

NORA: (*Looks at the clock.*) It is still not too late. Sit down, Torvald, we two have a great deal to talk about . . .

THE MASTER . OF CEREMONIES: Dear ladies and gentlemen! You all know Ibsen's "A Doll's House." The remarkable ending has had a disappointing effect on you as it has on us. It seems to us no mean literary feat to effect a change, and so we turned to a series of dramatists, both living and significant, with the request to improve the ending of this not altogether untalented play and bring it closer to humanity. At this time we should like to express our thanks to the respective authors for their amicable responses and will now introduce their work in succession. (*He steps back.*)

FIRST IMPROVEMENT—FRANK WEDEKIND

(*Helmer enters left, Nora enters right to face him. They speak in the modern fashion, disdainful of the world.*)

HELMER: What is this? Not in bed? You've changed your clothes?
NORA: Yes, Robert, I have changed my clothes now. I am abandoning your house forever now. I am bound to find someone with whom I can spend the night.
HELMER: Yes, you are bound to find someone.
NORA: Therefore I am going now.
HELMER: You're crazy!
NORA: My dear friend, if I were crazy, I would stay with you, but I have come to my senses, and therefore I wish to know no more of you or of the whole world, I am pulling out of the whole mess.
HELMER: And what direction will your travels take?—You really must be crazy!
NORA: No, Helmer, I am not crazy, on the contrary, I have come to my senses, and therefore I am now going to a madhouse!
HELMER: Nora! (*Stretching out his arms in yearning, imploring.*) Nora, take me with! . . . (*The curtain falls.*)

SECOND IMPROVEMENT—MAURICE MAETERLINCK

(*Helmer and Nora slowly cross from right to left, their gaze directed into the distance, speaking in a hyper-tense, enraptured way, in slow sing-song cadences with attentuated movements. Gradual accompaniment by an harmonium backstage.*)

HELMER: I see with a shudder that you have changed your clothes. I pray you go to bed!
NORA: (*A black veil over her head.*) No, I shall now abandon your dwelling.
HELMER: You will abandon it.
NORA: Into night and mist.
HELMER: Into night and mist. Oh horrors! And once you have

abandoned the dwelling, you will reach a dark passage, a dark, dark passage.

NORA: Yes—a very dark passage.—

HELMER: And hence to the steps—to the high marble steps. You know them indeed.

NORA: (*Trembling.*) Yes, I know them.

HELMER: And from the high, chiselled marble steps you will come to the dark hall, where stands the door, the great door.

NORA: Yes, the great door—And the door is open by day, and the glittering sunbeams fall in the granite inlaid hall, and play in a thousand colors, in a paradisical penumbra. (*Helmer utters a long-drawn sigh and stands enraptured.*) And a great many human beings pass through it by day, and they do not see how bright the hall is. (*Helmer pronounces a stifled cry of lamentation.*) Then what do we human beings see in any case? And what is really bright and what is not bright?

HELMER: (*Muffled and heavy, as if Fate is speaking from within him.*) But by night it is sultry in the wide hall, then no sunbeam shines within, and no human beings pass through it, then the great door is closed by night, and I have the key to it, and that you won't get.

(*Nora sinks with a long drawn-out cry of woe on the chaise longue. The curtain falls.*)

THIRD IMPROVEMENT—JOSEPH LAUFF

(*A patriotic verse drama in impassioned tone. Nora and Helmer enter from left and right.*)

HELMER: (*In heroic impetuosity.*) What is this? You have changed your clothes? You are not going to bed?

NORA: (*Heroically.*) No, Robert, I am leaving your house immediately now.

HELMER: (*Seizes a nearby umbrella, as if he wanted to draw a sword against Nora, fights down the turmoil in his breast, lets the umbrella fall like a sword and draws back.*) But is this indeed in earnest?

NORA: (*In an intense pose.*) Aye, aye, I go, and I can no longer stay with you.

HELMER: (*Suddenly.*) If it must be, then, if you can stay with me no longer, let us at least once more before we part offer one another a toast! (*Becoming ever more rapturous and impassioned.*) A toast to the King of Scandinavia! The King of Scandinavia and his family—long may they live!

NORA: Cheers!

HELMER: Cheers!

NORA: Cheers!

HELMER: Cheers!

NORA: Cheers!

(*The shouts of "Cheers" must follow one another in a quick, sharp tempo.*)

HELMER: And may his race flourish!

NORA: And increase!

HELMER: And prosper!

NORA: And be strong throughout eternity!

HELMER: Hurrah!

NORA: Hurrah! And may his posterity rule over the earth from the North Pole—

HELMER: To the South Pole!

NORA: From the Urals—

HELMER: To Kilimanjaro!

NORA: For eternity!

HELMER: Hurrah! (*Short pause. Clutching the umbrella with both hands, holding it up to heaven as if in supplication.*) Nora, can you really not be moved to stay with me?

NORA: (*Cold and stark.*) No!

HELMER: (*Sinking to his knees and crying out in despair.*) Nora! (*In the distance the majestic thunder of artillery fire can be heard.*)

NORA: No! (*Pathetically.*) The most wonderful thing must happen! (*Louder thunder of gunfire.*)

HELMER: (*In the highest ecstasy.*) And that would be?

NORA: (*Filled with a prophetic spirit, in a patriotic trance.*) That our prophecies for the King of Scandinavia come true!

HELMER: (*Raising the umbrella in raptures, grasping Nora's offered right hand, his virilely courageous gaze fixed forward.*) God grant it!

(*The music now strikes up a martial march. In the background the portières part, a bust on the pedestal, turned towards the audience, is glimpsed, surrounded by green foliage and Bengal lights are lit on both sides. To the sound of bells ringing, cannons firing, and fanfares the curtain falls calmly and majestically.*)

AMONG THE NUMEROUS ARTIST'S TAVERNS THAT SPRANG UP IN Berlin was *Das Poetenbänkel im siebenten Himmel* (The Poets' Broadside in Seventh Heaven), founded by poetaster Georg David Schulz in January 1902. Located in a wine restaurant open all night, it was nominally only for ''members'' to avoid censorship, but mixed its bohemians with businessmen, bankers, and bureaucrats. Seventh Heaven's first star was ''Marietta di Rigardo,'' a Berlin seamstress who performed a Spanish dance with castanets and married Schulz.

It was Frau Schulz who introduced her friend, the feminist poet Margarete Beutler (b.1876), to the cabaret stage. Beutler had published a slim volume of poems, *Pictures From North Berlin*, in 1896, which proclaims her ideal ''to be a tramp (*Tippelschickse*).'' At Seventh Heaven, in the persona of ''Revolver Mitzi,'' she sang and recited her own material, vilifying woman's oppression and glorifying a life of free love and nature worship. Beutler has been neglected partly because Bierbaum left her out of the first anthology of cabaret songs, regarding her as ''too emancipated.''

The Lady is a Tramp

(Eine Tippelschickse zu werden)

1902

by

Margarete Beutler

I was born on January 13, 1876 in Gollnow in Pomerania. I never felt any love for my kith and kin, so there's no need to give you their names. I was brought up by the most dependable of all nursemaids: the sun. Anything that ripened in me ripened with its help. One day it lured me out of my parents' house. I went without noticing where. In the woods of Bohemia I let my girl's body sun itself through and through, until it was ripe for love. My eyes were keen, I could discern in the comfortless shadows a myriad, more than a myriad, of tortured, exasperated creatures who, unlike me, had never had an instinct for the sun. At this time I took a boy to myself in pure, free love, for by temperament I was not created for wedlock . . .

My soul is weighed down by a cookstove gray,
A heavy gray cookstove with saucepans of lead,
My soul is weighed down by a broadsword blade,
The hilt embellished with boys' curly heads
And a motto: "Women, suffer and be still!"
My soul is weighed down by a mountain of bills,
And—oh God!—by a man's oppressive belly!
How can a woman endure all this?—tell me!

* * *

She lay on the steps by the open church door—
At long last happiness seemed in store,
At long last she felt by quiet assuaged—
No children were squalling, no argument raged.

She kissed something hot, ray of sunshine—
Then up she was yanked by a hand: You swine,
How dare you sleep off, you mis'rable louse,
Your drunken nights here at God's own house?

Then a cop was shaking her this way and that—
Her knees bent limply, heavy and flat.
She whimpered . . . her kerchief came undone,
The strands fell loose from her small brown bun.—

Around her scrawny neck danced her hair—
She wanted to scream out: it isn't fair!
I've lived a life full of thirst, pain, grime,
Today I got tipsy—the very first time!—

Her gullet with whiskey is raw and sore—
Her poor mouth can only gurgle and roar.
She hauls herself forward, each move a job,
Her steps are dogged by a howling mob.—

Her skirts shuffle meekly along the canal—
"To church," the holy bell starts to call.
And pious women flinch in dismay,
And shudder together and hasten away.

IF WOLZOGEN'S *ÜBERBRETTL* WAS TOO CONSCIOUSLY ARTY AND Reinhardt's *Schall und Rauch* too much an insider's haunt to be considered the first true German cabaret, that honor may fall not to Berlin but to the more conservative town of Munich. There the *Elf Scharfrichter* (11 Executioners) was established on 13 April 1900 by the writer and director Otto Falckenberg, the critic and poet Leo Greiner, and the student Marc Henry (actually Achille Georges d'Ailly-Vaucheret) who had been a conférencier at the *Lapin Agile* tavern in Paris.

This cabaret was a direct response to the so-called Lex Heinze (nicknamed for a convicted pimp), a tightening of the federal anti-obscenity legislation which objected to works or performances which "without being obscene, grossly injured feelings of shame . . . and morality." In a backroom of the Golden Stag inn, a small stage with a "sunken orchestra" was set up. The walls were hung with cartoons by such radical artists as Félicien Rops, Théo Steinlen, and the cartoonists of the satirical journal *Simplicissimus*. Also on the walls were the masks of the eleven executioners, for the founders and their friends came on as medieval hangmen with red cowls and axes, denominating themselves Dionysius Death, Chill Noose, Caspar Hatchet, Tyl Gore, Seraphim Sepulchre, and the like. Performances were billed as "Executions" and the one woman in the company, Marya Delvard, lent a gaunt vampiric presence, as she sang in uninflected sepulchral tones.

Intimacy was preserved by the limitation to eighty seats, and the macabre atmosphere was kept up by sophisticated lighting on a blue-gray cyclorama. The three weekly performances of a bill which changed every month were always sold out, for the level of artistry was extremely high. The satire was more cultural than political, but even so the police frequently intervened, complaining of indecency. This reputation for subversion and raciness derived in no small part from its choice of authors.

Ludwig Thoma (1867-1921), for instance, was in constant hot water with the censorship and courts during the Wilhelmine period.

In 1906 he would be tried and imprisoned for his poem "Away with Love" which attacked reactionary morality and appealed for artistic freedom. His cabaret parody of a meeting to protest British atrocities in the Boer War is a classic indictment of the narrowmindedness of the German middle-class.

Hans von Gumppenberg (1866-1928), the son of an impoverished Catholic nobleman, had once been sued for *lèse-majesté* when someone claimed the king in play of his was Wilhelm II; he was later imprisoned on the same charge on account of a poem. Since he was serving as theatre critic on a Munich paper when the 11 Executioners flourished, his parodies for the cabaret were written under the pseudonym "Jodok"; they include "The Neighbor," his brilliant compression of a Hauptmann naturalistic tragedy into one breathless sentence.

By far the most illustrious collaborator at the 11 Executioners was Frank Wedekind (1864-1918) who, after a wandering life as a journalist and (he alleged) secretary for a circus, settled in Munich, where he made a living off his plays and humorous sketches for *Simplicissimus*; in 1899 he served a six-month prison sentence for *lèse-majesté* in a poem about the Kaiser's trip to Palestine. Wedekind's close acquaintance with London music hall and Parisian *cabaret artistique* influenced the format of his works: as one critic remarked: "all life is for him a music hall performance."

Wedekind can be considered the first true chansonnier of the German cabaret, interpreting his own poems to lute accompaniment. ("Careful, the mandolin is loaded," as Klaus Budzinski was later to say.) Like Marya Delvard, his delivery was sharply accentuated, his mien impassive, his style sardonic. There was "true daemonism in him," wrote von Gumppenberg. Brecht recalled Wedekind's voice as "brittle, somewhat monotonous, and quite untrained: never before had a singer so shocked and thrilled me. It was the man's enormous vivacity, the energy which enabled him to defy sniggering and contempt and proclaim his noble canticle, that also endowed him with this personal magic. He seemed indestructible."

The relationship between the 11 Executioners and Wedekind before it closed in 1904 was a symbiotic one. He provided them with his trenchant ballads and their finest play, the pantomime drama *The Empress of Newfoundland*, and they paid him very good money.

The Executioners' Song
(Scharfrichterlied)
1901
by
Leo Greiner

(Chorus)   Stately towers the pitchblack block,
Our sentence sharp and sane is.
Blood-red our heart, blood-red our smock,
Our pleasure full of pain is.
Whoever does the day offend,
His last rites will be gory,
Whoever makes pale death his friend
Is hailed in song and story.

(Solo)   Deliriously Time's motley sand
Clings tight, in night to wind the land,
And so our beacons blazing stand,
On high their banners flutter.
We light this fast decaying ball,
Which scarce can one day's dark forestall.
May the mad God who rules us all
A cruel sentence utter.

(Chorus)   A shadow dance, a puppet play!
You bland and happy fellows!
Old God above maintains his sway
O'er puppets and o'er shadows.
He sways to bliss, he sways to grief,
On high the prayers take wing,
And just as they achieve relief
We amputate the string.

The Protest Meeting
(Die Protestversammlung)
1901
by
Ludwig Thoma

(*A hall in the "White Eagle" Hotel. Packed with members of the "German Oak" society. The members wear, if possible, old-fashioned frockcoats and top hats; most of them have umbrellas. Down right is the podium; beside it the chairman's table. At the table sits the executive committee: the rentier Röpke, the merchant Flosse, and a secretary. Röpke mounts to the podium amid general hubbub. The secretary rings a bell, whereupon silence ensues.*)

RÖPKE: (*Frequently clearing his throat.*) Highly respected members of this society! Gentlemen! As you may all be aware, the plight of Boer women and children in South Africa is a most critical one. These facts will reverberate, if anywhere, then in German hearts! (*A few muffled bravos! Hear, hear!*) Yes indeed, gentlemen, *reverberate*. We respond to this as Germans, we respond to this as fathers of families (*Bravos!*), we respond to this as German fathers of families. (*Lively bravos! Röpke grows more plangent.*) Two years ago when the war in South Africa broke out, a flame of enthusiasm was kindled in the heart of every German male, and it virtually blazed, virtually, gentlemen! (*Bravo!*) Need I remind you of the festivities we put on? Need I remind you of the family get-together in December 1899, of the punch bowl party in January 1900? (*Bravo!*) The names Modder River and Spionkop are inextricably connected with the schedule of our society's soirées. (*Very forceful bravos. A particularly en-thusiastic party at the back of the hall roars frightfully: Hurrah, hurrah, hurrah!—with the emphasis on the first syllable.*) We have never forgot that these brave heroes in South Africa have German blood flowing through their veins, that they are the flesh of our flesh, bone of our bone, that they too are descendants of those who at—,who at—,who in the Teutoburg Wood shook off the yoke of foreign rule. (*Lively calls of bravo. The excited party roars again: Hurrah, hurrah, hurrah!*) Gentlemen! The German people now behold the wives and children of its valiant kindred comrades whelmed in misery. Is our great moral indignation to eh—eh—ebb away in embarrassed silence on this occasion? Eh? Is it to ebb indeed? (*Bravo! Bravo! The excited party shouts: Hur-ray for Röpke!*) Gentlemen! I invite your suggestions as to how the "German Oak" Society should respond to this situation, to the miseries of these kindred women. I suggest: filing a formal protest, sending pecuniary resources, and convoking a people's convention to meet at the close of the Hague Peace Congress. Will you please offer your opinions on this? (*Lively applause. Bravos with hand-clapping.*)

MEINICKE OF THE CHAMBER OF COMMERCE: (*Rises quickly, requests the floor and goes to the podium.*) Gentlemen! Before we concern ourselves with the state of the Boer women, I should like to ex-press to the previous speaker and our respected executive com-mittee the thanks of all those present (*hear, hear*), thanks that to-day, as so often in the past, he has found the proper expression for our German thoughts and feelings. (*Stifled bravos. They all look at each other portentously and nod their heads earnestly.*) His thoroughly German words ring in our hearts, where they have found a joyous echo. (*He bows deeply to the executive committee which responds with even deeper bows.*) Now, gentlemen! To the matter in hand! Never and in no way must we forget that politics is not *our* business, rather it is none of our business. I therefore believe that our demonstrators must keep within judicious limits, which on the one hand obey the injunctions of reason, on the other hand comply with the code of conduct approved by the police. Gentlemen! We Germans are proud that the honor of the German name, the German flag, uh, proudly flutters in the breeze. (*Bravo.*) Yes, indeed, gentlemen, inside and outside, but we must be careful not to behave with blind enthusiasm like, for instance, the French. We are, thank God, a nation full of self-confidence. (*Bravo.*) The German eagle builds its eyrie safe and fast, and when it spreads its wings, it does so with judicious prudence, as suits our national character. (*Tumultuous shouts of bravo. The excited party roars again: Hurrah, hurrah, hurrah!*) Gentlemen! We are morally roused by a great many events in South Africa, but, gentlemen, this arousal, is it in accord with the laws? (*Murmurs.*) We should therefore, gentlemen, behave in a very German manner, I mean, with caution.

RÖPKE: I yield the floor to Wholesaler Flosse.

FLOSSE: (*A type of the newly rich parvenu.*) Gentlemen! Please allow an experienced businessman to make a few remarks. I am a German, a German through and through—but I am also a pragmatist. In all my commissions and omissions I have always kept one principle in sight. This principle says: (*Pregnant pause.*) What's in it for me? (*Murmurs. Meinicke shouts: Hear, hear.*) Gentlemen, I haven't done badly by this principle, as you may know. (*Applause. Meinicke shouts again: Hear, hear! Absolutely!*) I've worked my way up from the bottom. I started a business with three employees and today 200 jump when I wink. (*Bravo! Meinicke claps ostentatiously. The excited party at the back shouts: Filthy snob!*)

RÖPKE: (*Rings for order.*) Order, gentlemen! Let's have decorum!

FLOSSE: (*Carries on.*) Gentlemen! I ask myself what's in it for me in this protest demonstration? Answer: nothing! Nothing at all! (*Unrest. Oho.*) I want to tell you something: here's what's in it for me. The English will boycott us; even today I can detect the pernicious influence of the war on my branch office. Gentlemen! in private life we are careful not to drive away certain customers, why should it be different in public life? (*Murmurs. Absolutely. He's right. Meinicke shouts: True enough.*) Feelings are fine things. Feelings are all right, but . . . we shouldn't overestimate them either. Charity begins at home, our self interest comes first, and this self-interest imperiously demands that we all abstain from anything that could damage business. (*Calls of bravo.*) I am against any demonstration that could upset England. (*Violent applause. A few grumbles. The excited party roars: Filthy snob!*)

RÖPKE: (*Rings very loudly.*) I must once more energetically request decorum. I will permit no insults. I yield the floor to the representative of academe, Herr Professor Dr. Wernhardt.

PROFESSOR WERNHARDT: (*Prototype of a German philologist. Blond full beard. Eye glasses. Double-breasted coat à la Dr. Jaeger. Speaks very pompously and formally.*) Gentlemen! It was always the prerogative of German learning to be in harmony with national feelings. Since I treat the question raised today as an historian, I would like to investigate: (a) what influence spontaneous demonstrations have in themselves; (b) in general and (c) in this specific case? To (a) the question immediately obtrudes, have we in this case (d) a right in general? And if so, (e) wherein does it subsist? Not always, gentlemen, was the Germanic race as aware of its integrity as it might, could and ought to have been in view of specific factors. In the great current, which is the signum of the Indo-Germanic migration, flowing at a time the exact identification of which has even today split the world of learning into two hostile camps, a fluctuating movement was conceived, that now hither, now thither the strict lines of historical research . . . (*Lively impatience. Quiet! To the point! That's enough! To the point!*) (*Continuing.*) Gentlemen! Excuse me for this slight digression, but it is necesary to the understanding of what follows. Now, as I was saying, in this fluctuating movement the contours were so gradually obliterated that today we can scarcely establish with the precision which is a happy and never adequately appreciated prerogative of German research and the historical field in particular, where the boundaries of individual nationality are to be found. *At times* they sharply veer off from one another, *at other times* they blend to the point of indistinguishability and *at still other times* . . . (*The excited party shouts: And at still other times you'll shut your mouth, I hope.*)
RÖPKE: (*Rings.*) There is someone here who is evidently trying to go beyond the bounds of decent behavior. I warn the party in question to give it up. (*The excited party roars: He won't!*) Eh—eh! Please, Herr Professor, carry on.
PROFESSOR WERNHARDT: Gentlemen! And so I turn from the Indo-Germanic period to the no less noteworthy epoch of the mass migrations. Considered in detail they can be divided into (a)—(*Loud grumbling. That's enough! That's enough!*) Gentlemen, you are preventing German learning from taking part in this question. I shall submit, but I wish that to be understood.
RÖPKE: (*Occupies the podium.*) Respected committee! Members of the society! We are all grateful to the Professor from the bottom

of our hearts for that interpretation so full of clarity and intelligence. It is merely want of time that motivated certain gentlemen to call for an end to the debate. (*Quite right. Certainly.*) Be assured of our sincere admiration, which the brilliant representative of *German learning deserves.* (*Bows. Calls of bravo. The excited party roars: It deserves it all right!*) Gentlemen! I also thank the other speakers, who took part so pointedly in the debate. It is one of the many superior qualities of the German people that it is so willing to be instructed, (*Bravo!*) that it does not stubbornly cling to its prejudices. (*Bravo!*) Gentlemen, I believe we are instructed. (*Loud bravos.*) I should like to declare here and now that far be it from me and anyone present to give offense in any way at any time. I believe that although the demonstration I proposed would obtain the seal of approbation, the slightest doubt uttered in this regard has made me—and here I speak for everyone—(*Bravo! Bravo!*) I say, the slightest doubt has made me change my mind. I drop my proposal; I perceive that it has less to do with what we want to do than with what we may do. (*Quite right! Bravo!*) So, now, gentlemen, I believe that we should confine ourselves to expressing our sympathy for the unfortunates. I do not believe that we shall give offense thereby—or am I wrong?—(*Shouts: No, no! That's fine!*) We shall do so in a form which suits the habits of the German family, I refer to the picture postcard.

FLOSSE: (*Leaps up and shouts.*) Gentlemen! I advise you not to. I know the English national feeling. It won't stand anyone offending its pride.

RÖPKE: *We* are proud too. But if you believe . . .

FLOSSE: I don't *believe*, I *know.*

MEINICKE OF THE CHAMBER OF COMMERCE: Gentlemen! Let me make a compromise proposal. We ought to do something, the highly moral indignation that inflames us demands it, but we are cautious. England too has a sacred claim on our feelings. (*Bravo! Quite right!*) I propose that we send picture postcards, but . . . (*he looks around triumphantly*) with illegible signatures! (*Tumultuous sustained applause. They all raise their umbrellas and shout: Hurrah, hurrah, hurrah!*)

Translator's Notes

The Boer War (1899-1902), fought in the Transvaal between the British and the Dutch settlers, was remarkable, among other things, for the British introduction of concentration camps, which interned Boer civilians.

Modder River and Spionkop. Two battles in 1900. Spionkop was the site of a British retreat with heavy losses, the Modder River the scene of a battle leading to the relief of Kimberley by the British.

Teutoburg Wood. The location of a battle in 9 A.D. where Arminius (Herrmann) the German leader destroyed three Roman legions. It was considered by patriots the foundation of German nationhood.

Hague Peace Conerence. At the suggestion of Tsar Nicholas II, the first international peace conference was convoked at The Hague in 1899. It established the international court known as The Hague Tribunal, but could not reach agreement on disarmament.

Dr. Jaeger. Gustav Jaeger (1832-1917), German biologist and clothing reformer, who objected to the use of vegetable fiber in clothes. The "Jaeger suit," sported by G. B. Shaw, was a Norfolk jacket and plus-fours made entirely of wool.

The Neighbor
(Der Nachbar)
A Monodrama in One Sentence
1901
by
Hans von Gumppenberg

Groan not, great sorrows call for silence;
Nature's loquacious, art must be more meek!
Only lowly spirits talk a show of violence.
Genius shows itself in knowing when to speak.

SILENT CHARACTERS:

Gottfried Swallow, druggist
Susanna, his wife
Yetta, Lotta, Susanna's daughters by her first marriage
Fritz, Gottfried's presumptive son by his marriage to Susanna; a
   young merchant
Bodo von Spindle, Lieutenant, Lotta's fiancé
Rosa, maid-of-all-work to the Swallows

THE SPEAKING CHARACTER:

Franz Eberspacher, Registrar, the Swallows' neighbor

THE SCENE:

The parlor in the Swallows' house. At the back of the room
Swallow, Yetta, Fritz, Susanna, von Spindle, and Lotta are sitting on

chairs arranged in a semi-circle. Far right at a little table, near a massive, larger than life-sized wardrobe set against the wall, audience right, with a footstool in front of it, is the maid-of-all-work Rosa—knee-length skirt, white stockings—busy with a coffee-percolator. As the curtain rises, the seated characters are engaged in a calm and cheerful conversation, Swallow with Yetta, Fritz with Susanna, von Spindle with Lotta. Almost at once Eberspacher enters down left—in a shabby black clerk's frock coat, an order of merit in his buttonhole—he slowly takes a step into the room, removing his black top hat but not bowing, and stands to one side throughout the following sentence.

STAGE ARRANGEMENT:

NOTE:

The italicized words in Eberspacher's speech are meant as cues to be picked up by the silent characters, and not to be stressed as speech.

Eberspacher in a dry,
measured, passionless
tone, speaking more to
himself, without looking
at anyone present:
Although in wishing
you good evening,
I, as a mere neighbor, a peaceful
functionary, who, when it comes to
difficult situations in life, has
also proved to be a harmless and
accommodating man, of a
contemplative, may I say
philosophical, nature,
really have nothing material
to do here in person,
appearing among you as a
so to speak uninvited guest, a less
than welcome disturber of the peace,
although urged by an ir-
resistable compulsion, which
I quite rightly take to be
the holy voice of a clear
conscience, to appear amongst you
with that dignified composure and
Christian meekness, fraught with the
weighty earnestness of the moment,
here, at this abyss of
manifold and unheard-of corruption
which seems to be clad in dignity,
but in reality is decked out (to
speak pictorially) with deceptive
blossoms whose roots have soaked
up destructive poison, for
nothing in this world, not
consideration for my own physical
safety nor the fear of animosity,
calumny and future persecution
nor any particular idea of a
moralistic, intellectual, material or

Mute pantomime by the
silent characters
(who, on Eberspacher's
entrance, stand up in a
row in amazement).

Swallow stands up
Susanna stands up

Fritz stands up

von Spindle stands up
Lotta stands up
Yetta stands up

They all become uneasy
They all look around in
confusion, von Spindle
tugs nervously at his
moustache.

They all become more
uneasy and perturbed.

They all evince the
utmost perturbation and
turmoil.

even purely aesthetic sort
will restrain me from revealing the
truth, which has been carefully
concealed, suppressed for years in
mysterious obscurity, but which for
all its *criminal silence gruesomely*   *They all take a*
cries aloud to heaven, the truth   *step backward in*
about your whole family   *mounting fear.*
at last, and indeed, as you
may well grant, not publicly,
but indulgently, in the absence of
alien witnesses, and with the aim of
instilling wholesomely discreet shame
and a spirit of reformation, here in the
arena of so many *abominations*, by   *They all flinch*
clearly stating all the   *in shock and guilt.*
individual *facts* that are at   *They all flinch again,*
issue and with that pregnant   *even more violently, Su-*
brevity, which indignation at   *sanna and the three girls*
these occurrences as well as a   *begin to tremble, Susanna*
human pity also claiming its   *and Lotta have to sit down,*
due notwithstanding and neighbor-   *because their legs won't*
ly love would require of even a   *hold them.*
wrathful judge, let alone a
modest fellow-man and neighbor, who
only obeys the admonition of his cate-
gorical morality *to proclaim loudly*   *They all stare at him in*
and inexorably, that according to my   *anguish with bulging*
systematic, oft-repeated, well-   *eyes.*
weighed, irreproachable, precise,
indeed agonizingly executed, in
short, regrettably infallible
observations, which I am able at any
time to swear to before a *court of law,*   *Swallow crumples up;*
the godforsaken father of this   *they all stare at him*
family, Mr. Swallow the druggist,
has for a long time now carried on a
criminal relationship with his
elder *stepdaughter Yetta*, moreover   *Yetta casts herself in*

his second *stepdaughter Lotta*
has no choice now but to take the

cardsharp and bad check artist
Lieutenant von Spindle
for very definite reasons and as
quickly as possible

in marriage, that,
as ill luck would have it,

the son and heir, after having
embezzled from his unsuspecting
employer, who is unfortunately
not present here,
thousands, then stole out of his
father's safe, which was unfortunately
merely fire-proof, the already laid-
aside *dowry* of the Lieutenant's wife-
to-be, and on a business trip
with a female of easy virtue
frivoled away every last penny of it,
afterwards took the innocent child
which *the maid-of-all-work Rosa*
bore him in secret at a certain
spot not to be named and which
the two of them in collusion

despair on Swallow's
breast; Susanna, beside
herself, wildly shakes
her upraised fists;
Lotta convulsively grips
the Lieutenant's hands,
leaning on him for pro-
tection.
The Lieutenant crumples
up, Lotta pulls herself
wildly away from him,
and stares at him,
shaking her head as if
crazy, while Sparrow,
Susanna, and Fritz shake
menacing fists at him.
Lotta, overwhelmed,
collapses, half un-
conscious, on her
chair,
hiding her face in her
hands; Swallow and
Susanna raise cursing
hands against her.
Fritz doubles up;
Swallow, Susanna and
the Lieutenant stare at
him.
Fritz doubles up even
more.

Lotta, Swallow and
Susanna rush at Fritz
with upraised fists;
the Lieutenant holds
Lotta back.
Rosa doubles up.
They all stare at her;
she drops to her knees
and wrings her hands.

*murdered, cut in pieces and
threw in the river by night,*
which behavior on the part of this
young man seems only the more
understandable, since he
himself is the hereditarily
doubly-tainted fruit of an
adultery, which his *mother,
oblivious to shame,* carried on
with the deceased epileptic

*Everyone is horrified.
Fritz drops to
his knees with convul-
sive twitches.*

*Fritz stands erect at-
tentively, with a frantic
movement; his eyes
roll and flash wildly.
Fritz springs up
and stares at Su-
sanna. Simultaneous-
ly, Swallow surges at
Susanna as if berserk
and throttles her.
Fritz contemptuously
pries him away, so that
Swallow dashes against
the wall, rushes back,
brandishing a stiletto
at Susanna, stabs her
and then himself.
Swallow pulls himself
together again, gasp-
ing, takes two vials
of cyanide out of his
pocket and gives one
to Yetta; each drinks
the contents of his
vial and they drop dead
together.
The Lieutenant pulls
out a revolver, shoots
Lotta dead with one
bullet and himself
with another.
Rosa has simultaneous-
ly leapt on the foot-*

assistant to the druggist, so
that as you stand here, hardly
one of you has any *reproaches* to
make to the others, but rather a
general

human *indignation* must take root
in the neighborhood, such as

now motivates me as well to tell
you these *things* with some

energy at last,

whereupon I wish you all
heartfelt *condolences* and
good night.

*Whereupon he puts the black top hat
on again, coolly steps over the corpses
and with measured tread, as he
entered, exits left, as the curtain
falls.*

*stool to the wardrobe;
she pulls a rope out
of her pocket and
hastily hangs herself
on a clothes-hook,
kicking away the foot-
stool. As she hangs,
she sticks out her
tongue and kicks
her legs forcefully.
Rosa's legs kick
more slowly.
Rosa's legs stop
kicking, she hangs
stark and still.*

Note for the Director

Rosa's auto-hanging is to be effected technically by having one of the assistants backstage catch her at the waist and sides or under the arms with a rope or a cord, which—invisibly to the spectator—will be hung from a sufficiently strong hook screwed into the ceiling, while she herself simultaneously slings her rope (which for safety's sake has been half cut through) around her neck and kicks away the footstool with her feet.

The Aunticide

(*Der Tantenmörder: "Ich hab' meine Tante geschlachtet"*)

1902

by

Frank Wedekind

I've gone and I've murdered my auntie,
My auntie was feeble and old;
I was spending the night in her shanty
Where I ransacked her coffers for gold.

A great deal of gold she was storing;
I found it, along with her bonds,
Though I heard how my auntie was snoring,
My heart was unmoved by the sounds.

Should she wake, she would be disconcerted!—
On ev'ry side night hemmed me in—
My sharp dirk in her guts I inserted,
Auntie's snoring stopped making a din.

The gold was a burden to carry,
But Auntie was heavier far.
Clutching tight to her wattles, I buried
Her down in the deepest cellar.—

I've gone and I've murdered my auntie,
She was feeble and old, that's the truth.
But, Your Honor, of grace be not scanty,
And think on my promising youth.

THE OTHER IMPORTANT MUNICH CABARET *SIMPLICISSIMUS* (OR *Simplizissimus*) was opened on 1 May 1903 by Kathi Kobus. She had been a waitress at a poet's tavern called *Zur Dichtelei* (The Poetery); enjoined by law from calling her new enterprise the Neue Dichtelei, she got permission to use the name of the satirical journal instead. The habitues of *Simpl*, as it was affectionately known, were primarily painters, poets, and writers, including Gumppenberg and Wedekind, who performed their own material. Kobus paid them in food and drinks or by buying paintings, but gradually she began to hire specific performers and develop her own ''stars.''

Among these were Hanns Bötticher (1883-1934) who had knocked about as a cabin boy, a showbooth stagehand, a salesman for roofing material, and a window dresser. He was working as a tobacconist in 1909 when Kobus made him her ''house poet,'' a post he held until 1911. Bötticher's verses, nonsensical yet satirical, often hymned the exploits of able seamen Kuttel Daddeldu in an idiom half Kipling, half Lewis Carroll.

Kathi Kobus retired to her villa in 1912, but lost her money in speculations, and after World War I returned to the Simpl. She died in 1929. Bötticher ran a mine-sweeper during the war; after a volume of his poetry was published in 1919, he began to use the pseudonym Joachim Ringelnatz. Walter Mehring discovered him in Munich and brought him to Berlin where he sang at the Wilde Bühne and the second Schall und Rauch (see pp. 210-11).

Kathi Kobus and "Simplizissimus"

(from Mein Leben bis zum Kriege)

1931

by

Joachim Ringelnatz

One afternoon we were lounging along Turk Street. There we read a yellow poster on a restaurant door: "Simplizissimus-Artists' Tavern," illustrated with a red dog trying to uncork a bottle of champagne. Artists' tavern! Artists' tavern! Just what we were longing for! We ventured inside. In the sparsely lighted room the chairs were still piled on the tables. A waitress filled us in. Artists and customers never arrived before ten o'clock at night.

We turned up there again that night. The pub was full to the bursting, so that we had to stay in the front room. On the walls hung picture upon picture and at the tables sat guest upon guest, packed tight, mostly students. The landlady wore a peasant costume as she greeted newcomers and called everybody, us too, "Du." People called her Kathi. She was a stately woman and seemed extremely cordial.

A three-man band played Viennese songs. Then Kathi distributed the text to a Simplizissimus song that had been composed by Baron von Osten-Sacken. We drank punch and sank into a voluptuous mood. The next night after closing-time at work I hurried back there. The red lamps winked seductively and promisingly before the entrance, where a long row of private cars was drawn up. Again the pub was overcrowded. A narrow passage led to the back room. I managed to find a spot overlooking it. Artists, students, girls, elegant ladies and gentlemen. They sat narrowly squeezed around tables with white tablecloths. On one of these tables stood a slender man with a wild beard, piercing eyes, and elegant hands. He was reciting a poem. ''I was once a revolushner.'' I asked one of the students standing beside me who the reciter was. ''Don't you know? You ought to be ashamed!'' I really was ashamed. A rather elderly flowergirl who was moving around enlightened me. The gentleman on the table was the venerated anarchist Erich Mühsam.

On the third night I sat right in the back room. And from then on I spent every night and all my money there, although I ordered only the plainest drinks and sipped at my glass for a long time. The atmosphere was much too beautiful. It was stimulatingly beautiful. It was something entirely new to me.

Over time I became acquainted with the pub, its landlady, its habitués, I met thousands of people there.

The landlady in the Chiemgau peasant dress was named Kathi Kobus and was the child of peasants from Traunstein. She didn't always wear this outfit, but also appeared in an urbane, expensive wardrobe hung with precious jewelry. She always looked showy and alluring, so that a great many men and women fell in love with her, although at the time she was 55 years old and wore a wig. The artists who hung out there had urged her to open her own tavern. So she founded ''Simplizissimus'' and as poster earned herself the red dog so comically drawn by Th. Th. Heine.

Heine, Rudolf Wilke, Wedekind and other famous people hung out there, and younger painters, poets, and actors, some of whom later gained fame and money themselves. They all supported Kathi, insofar as they gave her pictures or paid their bills with them, designed decorations and filled the place with exuberant activity. ''Simpl'' was the focal point of Bohemia and became world famous. Anyone who lived or studied in Munich went there. Anyone passing through Munich visited Kathi. Yes, people came from America and other countries simply to meet her and her artists' tavern. The young artists sang to the lute or the piano. Others danced, put on scenes from plays, did magic tricks, every kind of artistic entertainment was on offer. At first it was improvised, later as Kathi made a lot of money by it, it was performed by contract and for a wage, although a very stingy wage. Even Wedekind performed there . .

In the backroom was the stage, a narrow platform with a piano on the left and an harmonium on the right. The piano was used by a long-haired factotum by the name of Klieber. Old Klieber hummed wonderfully to himself when he played. He also liked to drink and his favorite topic was chemistry.

"Simplizissimus" was crowded every day. When all the chairs were filled, Kathi knew how to create room for new customers. Stools were set up in the passages. "Please, squeege together a little!" Kathi would say in dialect. Whereupon she would imploringly put her hands together and let a madonna-like flutter of the eyes take effect. A minute later she would be in the kitchen cursing out an apprentice maid in the coarsest Bavarian Billingsgate. Her talent at organizing was matched by a reckless energy. The story went that once the German Crown Prince had gone to "Simpl" incognito and after closing time Kathi had said to him and a couple of other dalliers, "Git home w' ye, ye damned Proosian sonuvabitch." Frequently students who made a fuss when under the influence would be violently thrown out by Kathi single-handed.

. . . Kathi Kobus acted as mistress of ceremonies and strove for quiet. "Silence for Anna Trautner!"—"Knock it off!" She too performed, dialect poems by Julius Beck, and was unabashed at interrupting her performances with business remarks. "Anni, mind what you're about! The gent wants to pay!"—or, if she saw a new guest at the entrance: "Come on in, there's still a seat over here."

. . . One night I got up the courage to ask Kathi whether I might recite a poem. She was happy to oblige. "Silence, a customer is kind enough to recite us a poem."

I don't remember whether I had stage-fright as I crossed the platform and recited a couple of lyrics of my own. In any case it was a total flop. Only a pair of hands applauded out of compassion. I meekly crumpled up. But I kept going back to "Simpl" every night. A few days later, I made another attempt on the small stage, but again won no approval. This rankled me a lot. I composed a long comic poem, a take-off on the conditions of the tavern that included Kathi's stand-by phrase, "There's still plenty of room, keep on coming." I learned this poem by heart and performed it. The applause was tumultuous. Kathi's thanks was overwhelming . . .

Every night I performed the "Dream of Simplizissimus," as the poem was called. It was tumultuously demanded. I composed new topical verses for it. Kathi introduced me to Herr and Frau Scharf and the rest of the artists, and now I sat, as I had longed to, at the artists' table. Every night till about three o'clock. Hugo Koppel made a point of my not paying for the two steins of Magdalener I drank and later I even got a salary of one mark a day. To earn it I had to recite four or five poems twice. Now and then I would be treated by customers. That was the case with all us artists. Sometimes we would be swimming in champagne. A manager or agent from Deutz and Geldermann came. He had a commercial interest in running up a good bill for his brand of champagne. He had us artists served champagne not by the glass but by the bottle. And Kathi drank along. And the man from Central Australia drank along. Until we couldn't stand it any more. Then I hauled two full bottles into the kitchen. But the cook and the scullery-maid waved me away, for they too were full of Deutz and Geldermann. Koppel and I took time out. We wanted to treat the big spender to a thank-you. I hurriedly composed a little verse and Koppel intoned it in variations on the harmonium.

> If you're sad and something hoits,
> Drink up Geldermann and Deutz,
> If you're better later on,
> Drink up Deutz and Geldermann.

OTTO REUTTER (PFÜTZENREUTER, 1870-1931) IS A GOOD EXAMPLE of a performer who straddled the worlds of popular music hall and cabaret. He had toured with a folk-singing group before entering variety in Berne in 1895, and soon became the most popular comedian in the German-speaking world, his big break-through coming at the Berlin Wintergarten in 1899. He wrote and sang his own songs, over a thousand of them, expressing such sentiments as "It'll all be the same fifty years from now" and "Nothing surprises me no more." His patriotic conservatism was leavened by a witty turn of phrase that compressed a good deal into a few pungent words and proved a model for later, more satirical songwriters like Kurt Tucholsky. Reutter himself once remarked, "My main specialty is commenting on contemporary sensations and trends in the most dramatic form possible, so far as the censorship allows." More important, on a variety stage cluttered with stentorian voices and wink-wink-nudge-nudge comedians, Reutter's style was intimate, rapid-fire, and allusive, in short, cabaretic.

How To Be a Humorist
(Wie wird man Humorist?)
1910
by
Otto Reutter

Write your verses yourself. Nowadays everyone writes his own verses, even the people who don't write them themselves. It isn't hard. The end-rhymes don't have to be more than passable. If you rhyme ''Gustav'' with ''Gasthof'' that's perfectly all right. See to it that the last line of the couplet contains a little joke. It doesn't have to be brilliant, because the audience cares less than you think, and laughs at any nonsense. I know that from experience. During your act try to lend your face a real stupid look. You won't find this too difficult. I never found it too difficult. The audience, however, feels flattered for it thinks you're dumber than the people out front. Let the audience think so. You'll find it pays off. Don't sing anything whimsical—or anything witty either. People don't like that. Also avoid true humor too as much as possible and keep to the downright comic. People want to laugh, not smile. You see, I might be able to write verses which don't skim the surface so much; but the bulk of the audience doesn't like that. So I don't bother doing it. I believe my best verses are the ones I have *never* written. So try above all to achieve a really big laugh success and don't be faint-hearted in deciding how to do it. You see, nowadays every night at the end of my act I indicate that I don't want to sing any more by showing I'm already undressed, I toss my black trousers out of the wings stage right,—and people laugh at that more than my whole act. I wanted to make this splendid joke years ago, but you need *two* pairs of pants to do it, and I never had more than one before.

The Motley Theatre. Above, the interior from the back. Below, the usher- and front-of-house staff in the audience.

Ernst von Wolzogen as conférencier.

Silhouette of Kathi Kobus.

Opening night party for the Berlin Überbrettl. Seated Center is Ernst von Wolzogen with his wife on his lap.

The founders of Schall und Rauch: Martin Zickel, Friedrich Kayssler, and Max Reinhardt, with cigarette.

The Bad Boys: Carl Meinhard, Leo Wulff, Rudolf Bernauer, and Paul Schwaiger.

Bozena Bradsky and Robert Koppel rehearsing "The Merry Husband" with Oscar Straus at the piano.

Paul Schwaiger and Jenny Rauch in the Joseph Lauff section of Nora.

Paul Schwaiger and Jenny Rauch in the Maeterlinck section of Nora.

Margarete Beutler on stage.

The 11 Executioners.

The audience at the 11 Executioners.

Frank Wedekind with his lute.

Christian Morgenstern.

Joachim Ringelnatz performing at the Munich Simpl.

Otto Reutter. On his lap is the dancer Saharet, parodied at the Bad Boys cabaret.

Caricature of Marya Delvard.

III

THE ARTISTIC CABARET
IN
EASTERN EUROPE

1905-1916

POLISH CABARET SPRANG UP IN CRACOW RATHER THAN IN THE modern capital of Warsaw, because Cracow was both a crossroads of German-Austrian-French cultures and a seething patriotic center. A nest of intelligentsia, it housed a university and the Academies of Sciences and Fine Arts. The earliest suggestion of cabaret was the artistic coffee-house, the *Paon* (Peacock), of 1899. The Paon was a direct ancestor of the *Zielony Balonik* (Little Green Balloon), which opened on 7 October 1905 in a confectioner's shop, known as *Jama Michalika* (Michalik's Cave) because the shop was owned and operated by Jan Apolinary Michalik. At first it served as an art gallery, hung with the drawings of its patrons. The initiator of the Green Balloon was Jan Kisielewski, a comedy writer, but its presiding genius was the novelist and playwright Stanisław Przybyszewski, who had led an anarchic and bohemian life all over Europe. His unbridled example had a liberating effect on his stay-at-home contemporaries.

However, the most productive and effective writer for the Green Balloon was Tadeusz Żeleński (1874-1942), a physician who rejoiced in the English pseudonym Boy. Under his influence, what had been a painters' club became more literary; unlike the Chat Noir or the Motley Theatre, which had remained peripheral to the intellectual life of Paris and Berlin, the Balloon was soon centripetal to the artistic talents of Cracow. The Balloon's counterpart to the Chat Noir's shadow-plays was the *szopka* or nativity play, a medieval puppet-show used as a framework for topical sketches and songs that might go on all evening. The combination of folk-tradition with modernist forms was profoundly Polish, and the use of puppets to sing subversive verses ingenious. Chafing under Austrian domination, the writers and performers perfected an ambiguity which made sense to an audience trained to read between the lines.

The conférencier, known familiarly as Stasinek, was Stanislaw Siersoławski, a Sanskrit scholar; in the exclusively stag ambience, Teofil Trzciński played all the women, winning himself the sobriquets "primadonna" and "androgyne." The Balloon's participants would have a major influence on Polish theatre: Boy became an important theatre critic and sponsor of reforms in costuming and censorship; Leon Schiller developed into a leading director and Karol Frycz an innovative scene designer.

When the Green Balloon closed in 1912, the actor Arnold Szyfman (1882-1967) opened the Momus in Warsaw, in an attempt to make a commercial success out of what had been a bohemian venture. It managed to carry on as a miniature theatre for high society until 1918, and its example unleashed a torrent of similar enterprises, whose M.C.'s used the sacramental language of the *szopka* to mock at the audience and local abuses.

A Strange Adventure of the Połaniecki Family
(Dziwna przygoda rodziny Połanieckich)
1908
by
Boy-Żeleński

Carnival night in a respectable Polish home. From the next room come the strains of a waltz, the voice of the caller bawling the exotic names of cotillion figures, the rustle of gowns in the dance, etc. I was dozing off in a comfortable armchair; all of a sudden I caught a glimpse of something whirring by me as a belated couple tore past like a hurricane, and in their speed knocked over, horrors, a bottle of the finest old cognac, which I was saving for my private use. The worthy liquor began to trickle, inundating a splendid de luxe edition which lay appropriately and majestically on the table of this Polish house. I looked: it was *The Połaniecki Family*. I was gazing melancholically on the thick vellum boards, dripping golden fluid, when suddenly I thought I could hear distinct sounds, as if voices were issuing from the pages of the book:

* * *

"Mr. Stan!"
"What, Miss Marynia?"
"I wanted to tell you something . . . All of a sudden my head started spinning something awful . . ."
"That's funny, I felt it too . . . It must be the dancing."
"Mr. Stan . . ."
"What, Miss Marynia?"
"No, I'm ashamed . . ."
"I can't believe Miss Marynia could think of anything to be

ashamed of . . ."

"Mr. Stan is very good to think of me that way . . . but I'm not like that at all . . . somewhere deep, deep down I'm very depraved . . ."

"My dear child . . ."

"Mr. Stan . . . I would like to get married . . ."

"And so you will, Miss Marynia."

"I mean, right away . . ."

"My precious Miss Marynia, so would I, ever so much, I'd like you to visit my beloved estate once more."

"Oh, that stupid estate . . . boring hole . . . that won't do it . . . Oh, it's awful the way my head is spinning . . . Mr. Stan—"

"What, Miss Marynia?"

. . .

. . .

"Why doesn't Mr. Stan ever caress me or embrace me . . ."

"My dear Miss Marynia . . . my own, my very own . . . my own dearest child . . ."

"Not like that, Mr. Stan, hard, really hard, not the way you hug a respectable woman, but differently somehow . . . I'm not sure what I mean . . ."

"That's not permissible, Miss Marynia . . . A religious service is required . . ."

"Ah, that's right . . . a religious service . . ."

* * *

"Oh, oh, oh, oh." (*Sobbing*.)

"Marynia, my child, what's the matter, m-my ch-child (for some reason my old tongue's getting twisted. And my head's in a whirl. Must be a storm coming on)."

"Oh, oh, oh, Professor Waskowski, sir, I'm so unhappy." (*Sobbing*.)

"What's wrong with Miss Marynia? Cuddle up to the old professor. That's it, even closer . . ."

"Oh, oh, oh, Professor, sir. Stan doesn't love me . . ."

"What nonsense is Marynia talking? Stan doesn't love Marynia? He, not love the youngest of the Aryóws?"

"But he doesn't love . . ."

"What's got into this head today? . . . Who wouldn't love my precious child?"

"Well, Stan doesn't (oh, oh, oh). Besides, what would he love me for?"

"Hush! It's a sin to talk like that. What for? Oh, you, you, you. What for? For those beautiful eyes, for that pink little puss, that neck . . . and these breasts . . . and these hips . . . and these tiny feet . . . and these calves . . . you, you, you . . . you little Aryów, you little rascal . . . and the way she dolls herself up, all these laces, all these trimmings, all these panties . . . You, you, you little tease . . ."

"Professor, what are you doing . . . someone will see . . . my head is spinning so . . ."

"A storm's coming on . . ."

* * *

"Mister Stan?"

"What, Litush dear?"

"My head feels so strange . . ."

"Come here, pussy, sit on my lap . . ."

"And will Mr. Stan pet his pussy . . ."

"I certainly will, Litush."

"It feels so good with you, Mr. Stan! So nice! That's a garter. Mr. Stan, what are you doing . . . That's not allowed . . . that's not allowed, Mr. Stan . . . Mr. Stan! . . . and what if I told Aunt Marynia, what would happen then? . . . Ha, ha, ha! . . . you *do* look silly, Mr. Stan. I was fooling, I wouldn't tell, because I love Mr. Stan, and he's allowed everything. And I can do anything I want to, because I'm going to die young . . . My head is spinning like it was at the birthday party when I drank champagne . . . Mr. Stan, it feels so strange . . . so nice . . . you are so sweet, sir . . . What are you doing . . . Mr. Staaaaan! . . ."

* * *

The whispers and murmurs died down. Evidently the Połaniecki family dried out and recovered their mental equilibrium, momentarily shaken by the encounter with a few drops of old cognac. I arose from the armchair and felt my feet were somewhat wayward . . .

Translator's Note

The Połaniecki Family was a best seller by Henrik Sienkiewicz, which every literate Pole would have read. Stanisław Połaniecki, a young industrialist, was taken as a model of an intelligent Polish everyman. He goes to collect a debt from a rural relative and falls in love with his daughter Marynia. In Warsaw the young couple meet the 12-year-old Litka, who has heart disease; she makes Marynia promise to marry Stan and then dies. The newly-weds lead a cloudless existence on their family estate. Boy-Żeleński's joke is making these pure-minded, exemplary characters go berserk under the influence of brandy.

The Café Momus, Warsaw

(from *Labirynt Teatru*)

1964

by

Arnold Szyfman

I thought about starting my own theatre, even the most modest. I began searching for proper accommodations, but it wasn't easy at that time in Warsaw. During my search I came in fortuitous contact with the engineer Jabuk Jasiński, one of the directors of the telephone company, a wealthy man who had recently become leaseholder or perhaps owner of the restaurant on Theatre Square, a few steps from the Great Theatre. It was an excellent restaurant, but it temporarily fell out of grace with fashion, and Jasiński was willing to rent the premises for theatricals, unaware that the room was useless for that purpose. When we met he tried to persuade me to open a cabaret there, something like the Frolics or the Green Balloon. After thinking it over and examining the terrain, we came to an agreement.

I clearly stated that I could not participate financially in the venture, and the fees for writers, musicians, actors, and management as well as the costs of both cabaret and restaurant had to be adequately covered. Jasiński accepted those terms, we signed a contract, and at the end of October 1906 it was decided to open the cabaret on New Year's Eve.

I named it the *Café Momus*, borrowing the title of a humor magazine published in the 1820s under the editorship of Alojzy Żółkowski, a great actor of the National Theatre. This Greco-Warsavian name turned out to be a great idea and was quickly and easily popularized. It also implied that the cabaret would have a satiric character.

I could count on Boy in putting together the program, for I'd got close to him over the previous months. He gave me the right to use many of his numbers already performed at the Green Balloon. On the other hand, problems arose in trying to find a cabaret diseuse or female singer. The young actor Henryk Małkowski introduced me to a number of actresses, singers, dancers, and amateurs, but I couldn't decide on any of them, for they were operetta or vaudeville or opera—but not cabaret. Then one day he brought to the Momus office a young actress, Mary Mrozińska, who had a special kind of beauty and uncommon intelligence. She struck me as an interesting acquisition and I signed a contract with her right away.

Not only did Mrozińska not disappoint us, but from her first appearance at Momus she won great success as an actress, reciter, and singer. Musically oriented, she made up for the lack of a good voice with poignancy, excellent acting, and chic outfits. Soon she became the audience's and press's favorite. At first she was the only woman in the troupe and used to be called our "only daughter." . . .

A major feature of the program was appearances by the painter Miki Mikun, who was for a long time one of the most acclaimed artists of the literary cabarets of Paris and Berlin. Her part consisted in drawing caricatures and staging shadow plays with music or songs (by Alfred Lubelski). A different kind of graphic parody was presented by Stanisław Szreniawa-Rzecki, an amazing caricaturist, who showed his caricatures to appropriate texts that were recited or sung; they were full of surprises and often received with bursts of laughter and applause. One young painter Władysław Krassowski parodied with charm and excellent technique the dances of Isadora Duncan; he looked great in stylized costumes and gave wonderful predictions of things to come.

The room lacked a theatrical atmosphere and could barely fit 150 persons at the tables. On the other side of the auditorium was the cafeteria, kitchens, dressing rooms, and offices. The contracts specified that meals would be served only in the intervals between the numbers, but in reality it worked out differently which led to frequent conflicts between the performers and the restaurant management.

Every show lasted between two-and-a-half to three hours, and because we began after the regular theatrical performances, the end of our show with supper would go until dawn. I even remember nights when guests leaving Momus would be greeted out on Theatre Square by newspaper boys. The shows lasted even longer when some fun-loving crowd would show up at Momus and participate in the production so actively they would even come on stage with their own numbers; or when the M.C. would spot a celebrity from the arts in the audience, he would be welcomed with a speech, song, even a poem improvised in a few minutes by one of the poets sitting at the Momus staff table.

The Momus material (usually performed some thirty times) was distinguished by the fact that, besides sentimental and light songs, there were sharp, ironic, or satiric monologues, poems, and songs packed with current events. Among the most popular was "Smoke from a Cigarette" with music by G. Goublier and lyrics by Lucjan Konarski, whose final stanza goes:

Life's a house of cards, love's a stupid joke,
Not even worth a cigarette's smoke.

Equally popular were songs on rather sad, sometimes macabre themes, such as "Wind Outside the Window" by Leon Schiller:

The wind outside the window jeers,
Damn it, life is full of tears,
No, I should give up the drink,
Tomorrow I'll change my life, I think.

The first program was supposed to be a revue of current events and happenings woven into a reception at the home of a popular Warsaw celebrity, of course properly disguised, but in reality the honorary Persian consul. This reception or ball at the Persian consul's might have given us an opportunity for lots of jokes, jests, and malice directed at the life of Warsaw's upper classes: social, artistic, and diplomatic. Unfortunately, the censorship completely wrecked this alluring plan and only tiny fragments found their way onto the stage. That's how we lost what was so far the most interesting part of our program.

In disputes with the censorship my situation was especially precarious, as a so-called "Austrian citizen" living in Warsaw for just a few months at a time and unable to speak a word of Russian. In one revue a few elegant gentlemen appeared in collars and ties but without heads. Why without heads? This detail made the Warsaw censorship a bit uneasy. Evidently if there are no heads, then who knows, maybe the censors missed a trick, maybe they're supposed to be Russian officials.

To find out, the chief of the secret police, Colonel Zawarzin, came to the revue and listened from start to finish. You could sense in the air not only the presence of Zawarzin but also that of a gang of secret agents. This visit, thanks be, had no repercussions.

There were lots of difficulties over the program "Old Warsaw": the police and censorship insisted that Momus held a cabaret permit which did not permit staging theatrical plays. This argument (suggested to the police—we suspected—by the Directors of State Theatres, who hadn't taken kindly to Momus from the first) was repeatedly used against our bigger stage acts.

The auditorium at Momus could not fit everyone who wanted to get in, and besides, not everyone could or would waste the night and money on a ticket and expensive meal at Momus; so charities took advantage of that fact and asked us to perform our show in bigger spaces in the early morning and afternoon hours, such as in the large auditorium of the Philharmonic. Even Momus itself began scheduling two shows on weekend nights to deal with the spill-over from weeknights. There was no end to these shows. Things came to such a pass that, despite significant income from these shows and concerts, the artists and staff had to refuse many offers, because the night shows were tiring everyone. And most of all me, who had never had a penchant for night or restaurant life. Despite all my successes, there came a time, at the height of Momus's popularity, when I decided to quit. I made that move after fifteen months. As Jerzy Zaruby writes in his memoirs,

> although it was a night club—since the show started at midnight and people sat at tables—it was carried on at a very high level in all respects. In spirit akin to Cracow's Green Balloon and small Parisian theatres of the type, its program reflected the spirit of the times: latter-day romanticism, suggestive atmosphere, and melancholic pessimism, finding salvation in grim cynicism. When Szyfman left, Momus soon ceased to exist. The later creations, Swiss Valley Gremlin and Mirage on Marszalkowski Street, were never up to Momus's level.

RUSSIA HAD A RICH TRADITION OF FOLK PERFORMANCE, BUT ITS experience of music hall and variety was exported from Western Europe and never seemed indigenous (indeed the words *myuzik-kholl* and *kafè shantan* reveal that). Like the Schall und Rauch, the first Russian cabaret arose from a theatrical milieu.

A. R. Kugel, influential editor of the journal *Theatre and Art*, and his wife the comic actress Zinaida Kholmskaya opened a "theatre of miniatures," the *Krivoe Zerkalo* (Distorting or Crooked Mirror) in 1908 in an ex-gambling casino in St. Petersburg, as a midnight show to follow Meyerhold's *The Strand*. Influenced by Wolzogen, Kugel saw the need to "fracture the theatre into its primary elements, to compress and condense it." He scrapped the conférencier and set out to parody the excesses of contemporary playwrights and directors. His first big hit was *Vampuka* by Ehrenberg, a lampoon of Italian grand opera. As the actor Khodotov recalled, on the eve of the Revolution, the Crooked Mirror "brought out all the incoherence and absurdity of our everyday life. It lashed out at obtuseness, conceit, smugness. It mocked at all the sanctimoniousness and hypocrisy of bureaucrats of all ranks and always urged and egged us on."

It was not until 1910 when the Crooked Mirror moved to the 750-seat Catherine Theatre, playing during standard performance hours, with the young dramatist Nikolay Nikolaevich Evreinov (1879-1953) as artistic director, that it really took off. Evreinov had alrady made a reputation as head of the Theatre of Yore, recreating medieval performance styles; and as the proponent of monodrama and "theatricality." The fourteen plays he wrote for the Crooked Mirror included a version of Gogol's *Inspector General* as staged by five different directors; an attack on ultra-naturalism called *The Fourth Wall*; and a monodrama set inside a lover's psyche, *Backstage at the Soul*. His favorite device was to present the same situation in several different modes, for he enunciated the notion that a director's work might be copyrighted as a writer's work is. *The School for Stars* is an attack on the competition, variety theatres that gave themselves airs as art houses; it was first produced in 1911 as an "episode from the life of Evreinov's kitchenmaid" (the version translated here is the revised one performed in 1922 at the Crooked Jimmy cabaret).

Evreinov's collaborators included Boris Fyodorovich Geyer (1876-1916), an ingenious comedy writer. Geyer's *Evolution of the Theatre* offered a love triangle as treated by Gogol, Ostrovsky, Chekhov, and Andreev; *The Water of Life in 4 Carafes* had a stage full of characters getting progressively drunker and the stage-set changing to reflect their perceptions; *What They Say, What They Think*, a reversal set-up that foretold Eugene O'Neill; and *Memory*, a *Rashomon*-like situation in which each of the participants in a domestic wrangle recalls the event with himself as protagonist. *Popular Fiction* is a shorter, but no less typical example of Geyer's playing with contrasts, as he juxtaposes a "Harlequin Romance" of the day with the squalor in which it was written.

Teffi was the pseudonym of Nadezhda Aleksandrovna Buchinskaya (1876-1952), daughter of a Petersburg professor. (She got her nickname "Taffy" from Kipling.) Her poems and sketches had appeared in the comic journal *New Satyricon* between 1906 and 1917, demonstrating her skill at parodying symbolist imagery and meter. Her Crooked Mirror skit translated here cleverly uses lantern slides to mock down-market lecturers. Like Evreinov, she emigrated to France after the Revolution.

The annual "cabbage parties" of the Moscow Art Theatre, when its normally staid actors would cut all sorts of capers, devolved into *Letuchaya mysh* (The Bat), created by the actors Nikita Baliev and N. L. Tarasov on 31 October 1910. Originally, it was an in-house operation, the first performance featuring a marionette parody of *The Blue Bird* with puppets of Stanislavsky and Nemirovich-Danchenko as Tyltyl and Mytyl seeking the blue bird of art. Affected by the World of Art movement, The Bat began to stage short stories, poems, and folkloric subjects with gorgeously stylized and colored sets and costumes, and Baliev as the genial, moon-faced host.

Brodyachaya Sobaka (The Stray Dog) opened in a wine-cellar in Michael Square, St. Petersburg, on New Year's Eve 1911, under the aegis of Evreinov, Kulbin, and Boris Pronin. Pronin, who had played a leading role as dramaturg at Meyerhold's experimental Interlude House, was the conférencier. In the two small rooms decorated with panels by Sudeikin, a hundred persons could be packed, from the time the cabaret opened at 10 p.m. till it closed at 4 or 5 in the morning. The clientele were classified by Pronin as either devotees of art or ''pharmacists,'' his term for philistines; and on Wednesdays and Saturdays, they all had to wear paper hats.

Although many of the habitués were Acmeist poets, among them Anna Akhmatova and Nikolay Gumilyov, no aesthetic agenda was paramount. The cabaret's anthem was written by the decadent poet Mikhail Kuzmin, who also composed a nativity play for Twelfth Night 1913. Often The Stray Dog housed celebrity events, as when the ballet star Tamara Karsavina returned from abroad and the futurist Marinetti paid a call.

The description of The Stray Dog set forth by the French writer Blaise Cendrars (1887-1961) in his novel *Le Plan de l'aiguille* is anachronistic, since he dates it 1904, seven years before the cabaret was founded, and a time when the tango had not yet come to Europe. His own work had been cited in a lecture at the cabaret, and his vivid description gives an impressionistic sense of the heady atmosphere that prevailed there. The Stray Dog was replaced in 1916 by *Prival komediantov* (Comedians' Rest), organized by Boris Grigoriev, Meyerhold, Pronin, and Sudeikin; and Sudeikin tried to recreate it in New York in 1924, as The Cellar of Fallen Angels.

The School for Stars

(*Shkola ètualov*)

Grotesque Parody in One Act

1911

by

Nikolay Evreinov

CAST:

The Headmaster of "The Music Hall School of Vocalism"
Instructress
Manager of the Music Hall
First, Second, and Third Baby, a trio
Servant
Apache
Apache Girl
Duncan Dancer
Music Hall Singer
Annushka

A mass of blaring, garish posters and photographs of stunning ballerinas. Downstage a small platform-stage. Left by the upright piano a tiny orchestra of "seedy-looking musicians." The "co-eds" cluster right. On the platform-stage is the "Baby Trio." Before the platform stand the Headmaster himself and an instructress. The conductor of the orchestra, who accompanies them now on the fiddle, now on the piano, is much out of sorts and often utters bitter truths to the musicians, whose faces show that they may make an effort but they are definitely underpaid. At the rise of the curtain, the Headmaster is beside himself. He is a very proud man, not devoid of "ex-

oticism'' in appearance, who speaks with a foreign accent and, like all poetic and talented natures, has unlimited impatience.

HEADMASTER: (*Bawls.*) Not like that, not like that, damn it! . . . How many times do I have to tell you, you accursed devils! . . . A one-year-old would understand that if you lift your right leg, you have to go down on your left. Did you learn that in a laundry?—then why bother coming to my school? I won't be compromised. (*Claps his hands.*) From the top! . . . (*To the musicians.*) Hey! . . . (*To the Babies*) Now let's have a smile, damn you! . . . Smile! You're not going to a funeral. If your auntie or your granny died, then go and pray, but don't try my patience.

INSTRUCTRESS: (*To the Babies.*) That's it, nice big smile! I said: smile. Lightly on the right foot! Nod your heads!

HEADMASTER: (*Bawls, claps his hands.*) From the top. (*The music plays.*)

BABY TRIO: (*Sings and dances.*) ''With cakewalks and maxixes, we were bored to tears in no time, but now a new dance craze appears. The Pola-pola's really blazing, the Pola-pola's just amazing. Everybody, small and tall, does this dance at every ball, it's the greatest fun of all . . . The Pola-pola sets you free, gets you into ecstasy. Don't we always take the tone set by modern Babylon? That must be the reason why we all give this dance a try. The Parisian's a patrician, 'cause dancing's his strong suit, he's won ev'ry competition and doesn't give a hoot!'' (*They dance to the music between the verses.*)

HEADMASTER: (*Stopping them.*) Stop! First I can see you don't understand a word of what you're singing. (*To the Instructress.*) Klavdia Ivanovna, did you explain the meaning to them?

INSTRUCTRESS: Good grief, Henrik Oskarovich, a thousand times at least. You know how devoted I am to my work.

HEADMASTER: Yes, but they sing as if it was nothing to do with them.

INSTRUCTRESS: (*To the Babies.*) Where is your phrasing, you heathens? . . . Didn't I show each of you individually, that . . .

HEADMASTER: (*Interrupting.*) I simply don't know what to do . . . The manager of the Variety Theatre will be here any minute—I promised him the trio would be ready:—he's got at most two numbers for the closing. He'll say I'm a fraud.

INSTRUCTRESS: (*In tears, to the Babies.*) I'm asking you, where is your phrasing?

HEADMASTER: (*To her.*) You should have asked that earlier, not now with a debut staring us in the face.

INSTRUCTRESS: Henrik Oskarovich, I really don't stint on energy.

HEADMASTER: (*To the Babies.*) Do you or do you not realize you're singing like cows? (*They are silent.*) What is this music hall ditty about? . . . Answer me . . . (*They are silent.*) Zhiguleva! . . . What is it all about?

ZHIGULEVA: (*One of the "trio," timidly.*) Uh . . . well, pola-pola means like it's sort of a fashionable dance, and the French do it, I mean, the pola-pola, they win contests with it . . . and don't give a damn, I guess.

HEADMASTER: And that's all?—Very clever. Remarkable. I see you don't understand even a word of what you've learned by heart—your sacred obligation.

ZHIGULEVA: For heaven's sake, Henrik Oskarovich: "With cakewalks and maxixes we were bored to tears . . ." (*Recites it to the end.*)

HEADMASTER: (*Unusually instructive.*) "With cakewalks and maxixes we were bored to tears"—then show that you're fed up with them, you're bored to death, you're yearning . . . "And now a new dance craze appears!"—it's a surprise!—act as if you're happy. Or for example: "Don't we always take the tone set by modern Babylon?" What's Babylon? Answer me. (*They are silent.*) Sidorova . . .

SIDOROVA: (*One of the "trio."*) It's a city.

HEADMASTER: What kind of city?

SIDOROVA: Babylon.

HEADMASTER: Well, what exactly is Babylon?

SIDOROVA: I just told you—a city.

HEADMASTER: (*Laughs contemptuously.*) It's Paris! . . . (*They are amazed.*) Paris. Paris is called "The Modern Babylon."

SIDOROVA: I never heard that. How was I supposed to know?

HEADMASTER: Then you should have figured it out. Why did God give you a brain? Answer me.

SIDOROVA: Paris. Now I know.

HEADMASTER: Well, and what is Paris?

SIDOROVA: It's the modern Babylon.

HEADMASTER: Do you understand now?

BABY TRIO: We understand, Henrik Oskarovich.

HEADMASTER: (*To the Instructress.*) Why didn't you explain it to them?

INSTRUCTRESS: I did explain it to them, but they forgot.

BABY TRIO: No, Klavdiya Ivanova, you never said a word about modern Babylon.

INSTRUCTRESS: You bare-faced liars! I even mentioned the Whore of Babylon.

BABY TRIO: You did mention whores, you were wondering which of us was a whore, but nary a word about Babylon.

HEADMASTER: Let's proceed! . . . "Don't we always take the tone set by modern Babylon? That must be the reason why we all give this dance a try." Understand?

ZHIGULEVA: Sure, because it's Paris.

HEADMASTER: Thank God. Then comes a period and you go on singing as if it were a comma. Klavdiya Ivanovna, did you explain to them the difference between a period and a commma?

INSTRUCTRESS: Not in the first verse, but in the second I even drew them and made them draw them.

HEADMASTER: Yes, but you're always too theoretical, Klavdiya Ivanovna. We don't intend to found a chair of grammar and punctuation. From the top! And legs higher, higher!—I won't be compromised . . . Let's begin! And smile, damn you . . . (*The Baby Trio sings and dances.*)

HEADMASTER: (*Interrupting the finale of the interlude music, leaps on the platform angrily.*) Sidorova!!! Gone wrong again? How many times do we have to rehearse this?! And why the hell are your shoulders always up in the air? Get 'em down, what an idiot! (*Pushes down her shoulders so that she screams and howls.*) Damn you! You want to put me in my grave. I won't be compromised. (*Comes down from the platform and wipes the sweat off with a handkerchief, as he toys with a multi-carat diamond.*)

INSTRUCTRESS: (*Consoling Sidorova.*) There, there, isn't she the cry-baby! Foo! So touchy! It's your own fault, getting all weepy like this.

SIDOROVA: (*Crying.*) I'm not an idiot, I can't help it if my shoulders are made this way . . .

ZHIGULEVA: (*To Sidorova.*) Oh, stop bawling! You got to put up with a lot for your art. Art demands sacrifices.

HEADMASTER: (*Clapping his hands.*) Interlude music! (*The orchestra plays the music, the Babies dance. At the end of the number.*) Zhiguleva! . . . Hmm . . . you said you had a sharp pain in your armpit?

ZHIGULEVA: Yes . . .

HEADMASTER: Klavdiya Ivanovna, be sure you tell 'em in the costume shop . . . what kind of fitting did she have? I'm fed up to here with measurements like that . . . Yes, Zhiguleva! (*He beckons with his finger, she comes down from the platform. In an undertone.*) Don't come tonight: there's something wrong with my stomach.

ZHIGULEVA: That's because you refused to put on your bellyband last time, you were being vain . . .

HEADMASTER: No, it's just some fish I ate. Arepina always stuffs me with all kinds of rubbish at dinner.

ZHIGULEVA: The bitch!

THE REST OF THE BABIES: Can we go?

HEADMASTER: Go on. Next! . . .

INSTRUCTRESS: Urykina!

(*The Baby Trio exits. A serio-comic in traditional costume comes on the stage.*)

HEADMASTER: Fixed it?

URYKINA: Yes . . .

HEADMASTER: (*To the musicians.*) All right!

URYKINA: (*Sings.*)

Once beautiful Katrina
Was walking down the track.
As soon as folks had seen her,
They laughed behind her back.
Through the dress she wore
Stockings showed their traces,
So did ribbons and laces,
And something more.

A young blade having seen her,
His admiration grew,
For beautiful Katrina
His passion was true blue.

On the spot he swore
Katrin he did adore,
For her his heart was sore,
And something more.

SERVANT: (*Entering.*) The new girls are here . . .

HEADMASTER: Klavdiya Ivanovna, see to them, angel!

INSTRUCTRESS: Right away. (*She hurries off left, followed by the servant.*)

HEADMASTER: (*To Urykina.*) Do you have a sharp pain anywhere?

URYKINA: No, nowhere.

HEADMASTER: Your feet are free?

URYKINA: (*Lifting her feet.*) Yes.

HEADMASTER: Then come over here! (*She does so. In an undertone.*) I'm free today too. Come by this evening.

URYKINA: Yesterday you said there was something wrong with your stomach? . . .

HEADMASTER: It's gone . . .

URYKINA: (*Laughing.*) Ah, what a sly fox!

HEADMASTER: (*Sternly.*) Now don't forget!—The school is a temple! . . .

(*The Instructress enters with two new girls: one is flashily dressed, the other wears a kerchief. The Headmaster looks them over pompously.*)

HEADMASTER: Third verse! Music! . . . Introduction! (*Claps his hands.*)

URYKINA:
Beautiful Katrina's
Agreed to be his wife,
But soon her misdemeanors
Make wretched his young life.
Three fellows pop indoor,
And hubby does, alack!
Hear one smack, second smack,
And something more . . .

HEADMASTER: (*Self-importantly.*) The treatment is by and large correct. Evidently you've been working on what I told you to. However certain minor details of the phrasing of the refrain are too crude. More psychology! I conjure you by all that's holy: more psychology! Don't skimp on the psychology. Don't spare it! It's the most important thing. And then the rhythm. Rhythm, rhythm, and more rhythm. You have to perform a religious rite when you sing a music hall ditty. Just what is a music hall ditty? (*Addressing himself more to the others than to her.*) Many people think that a music hall ditty is something like . . . Rooty, tooty, one, two, three . . . Not at all. The audience that comes to hear a music hall ditty requires aesthetic relaxation. Businessmen, bankers—do they come after a hard workday to see some Shakespeare, Uriel Acosta, and the like? Never. They see too much drama all day long. They don't need drama. Do they go to comedies?—no again. Where does such an audience go? They go to the cabaret. (*Laughter.*) And that's not a laughing matter, because here they get a well-deserved rest, here they can recuperate their strength for the morrow, here they see grace, wit, good clean work, in short, everything they never see at the office! . . . I implore you in the name of the highest goals, give them something first class! Take your business seriously. I beseech you not for your own sake, but for the welfare of the nation! (*The bystanders applaud.*) In particular, Comrade Urykina, you must make the refrain more piquant, and the interlude more rollicking. (*Leaps on the stage.*) Music! (*The musicians pull themselves together.*) Besides, you don't sing the verse about Katrina's lovers comically enough. You perform it like this. (*He sings.*) ''Three fellows pop indoors and hubby does, alack! hear one smack, second smack.'' That isn't funny. But this way it is funny. (*He shows her: everyone utters a forced laugh.*) The audience will split their sides. Understand?

URYKINA: I do. Thank you, Henrik Oskarovich.

HEADMASTER: That's right. Now, make me an exit to applause! (*She does so.*) Hmm . . . W-well, if you want to get sparse applause, that's the way to make an exit! But if you want the whole house to shake with the thunder of the plaudits then you should do it like this! (*He shows her. Urykina thanks him and leaves.*)

INSTRUCTRESS: Headmaster, please meet the new girls.

HEADMASTER: (*Self-importantly.*) Do we have a vacancy?

INSTRUCTRESS: Just two.

HEADMASTER: (*To the new girls.*) What genre do you practice? (*They are silent.*) What do you wish to specialize in? (*They are silent and ponder.*)—Serio-comic singer, lyrical soprano, quick-change artist, tramp comic, eccentric dancer, flamenco, living pictures, gypsy ballads, babies, Isadora Duncan style . . .

DUNCAN DANCER: That's the one.

HEADMASTER: Duncan style?

DUNCAN DANCER: Duncan or an American dance with my own negroes.

HEADMASTER: All our "my own negroes" have already been distributed. But if you're willing to go on without "my own negroes." . . .

DUNCAN DANCER: No, then Duncan.

HEADMASTER: Fine. (*To the shy one.*) And you?

ANNUSHKA: I don't know diddlysquat, sir. But I heard tell if a body gets in the show business, you just sing and dance and make good money at it—I mean, that's what Cook read me out o' the papers—I'm working my way up as scullery-maid in a restaurant—that they learn you that kind of stuff here, and give references besides and recommend a body for a job, so I came to give it a look-see and learn something too, check out the odds.

HEADMASTER: (*Thoughtfully.*) You read it in the papers? (*Smugly.*) Yes, yes, lots of papers mention our establishment.

ANNUSHKA: In the ads, I mean . . .

HEADMASTER: Ah yes, well, it's the same thing. Now then, let's see, the lessons will begin at once. Twenty million for the course and 25% of your salary when you go on the stage. Only you'd be wrong to think it's easy to become a music hall star! You need long schooling, serious work, inflexible principles. On the other hand, of course, a successful star can live like a millionaire. (*Points at the posters in turn.*) These are students of mine who graduated with a degree!—Fanny Edward!—international dances!—has 50,000 in gold in the World Bank, not to mention dresses, jewels, and so forth. Eleonora Tremblinskaya! the Polish diseuse, has an estate, foreign currency, a sealskin cape, and so on. Olya Lastochkina!—Russian serio-comic—kept by the ex-oil industrialist Galkin—wants to go to America and has already paid twenty gold rubles for a passport. Clara Fisher!—quick-change artist and music hall song-stylist—she died recently, the funeral alone cost her over two hundred silver rubles . . . Others of that ilk . . . So you go register at the office—three ruble fee, and we'll give you trial lessons immediately. (*Exits left.*)

APACHE: (*Rushing up to the Headmaster.*) But when do we do our apache dance? You promised you'd look at it on stage soon.

HEADMASTER: Right away, right away. Just give me five minutes, (*whispers in his ear*) nature calls. (*He is gone, with the apache behind him.*)

INSTRUCTRESS: (*To the flashily dressed one.*) If you please! (*Points to the platform-stage.*) You want to dance like Duncan? The most important thing for that is to take your shoes off.

DUNCAN DANCER: (*Simpering as she sits down.*) Ugh, that's awful. (*Takes off her shoes.*) Stockings too?

INSTRUCTRESS: How else? If you want to move like Duncan, away with stockings: it's a convention.

DUNCAN DANCER: (*Doffing them.*) Ugh, it's cold!

INSTRUCTRESS: (*Going up onto the platform with her.*) Please, here is a pin, tuck up your skirt and do what I show you. (*Suddenly stares at her feet.*) Have you got corns?

DUNCAN DANCER: It's my shoemaker's fault . . .

INSTRUCTRESS: Yes, but if you've got corns you should go to a pedicure first. Give me your word of honor you will see our pedicure this very day. 24 Marat Street,—say you're from our school.

DUNCAN DANCER: Yes, ma'am.

INSTUCTRESS: (*Displaying "beauty."*) First pose:—"striving for the ideal" . . . Pull in your elbows. Weaker in the knees. That's it. Second: "I will not accept this sacrifice." Pull back. You have localized obesity. Better get a massage. It's indispensable. Third pose: "I worship you, my beloved." More expression. Personify beauty. Hands down. God, what bunions! Don't forget: 24 Marat Street. From the top. "Striving for the ideal." That's it. "I will not accept this sacrifice." "I worship you, my . . ."

HEADMASTER: (*Entering with the apaches.*) But if you dance out of tune again, I'll tell you again, you're dancing out of tune.

APACHE GIRL: What about me?

HEADMASTER: You? . . . Ah, I did want to tell you something (*Leads her aside, in an undertone.*) For God's sake don't come today: for the last two days now, God knows what's been going on with my stomach—aches, pains. The doctor said, "absolute quiet."

APACHE GIRL: If that's what you want.

HEADMASTER: (*Clapping his hands.*) Klavdiya Ivanovna, let us have the stage. (*The Instructress and the Duncan Dancer step down off it.*) Music for the "Apache Dance!" (*The apaches dance their dance. The Headmaster marks the tempo with his foot and shouts:*) Cleaner! More precision! More sadism! Sadism! I beseech you, more sadism—that's where all the impact is . . . Expression! Psychology! Don't forget the psychology.

APACHE GIRL: (*Screams.*) Ay! He's pulling out all my front hair!

HEADMASTER: (*To her.*) Don't make a misstep. Keep in time. One, two . . . Psychology. (*At the end of the dance.*) If I tried to show you all your flaws, it'd take a week just to list them . . . First, dear girl, you have far too little shamelessness. If you want to pose as an innocent, get thee to a nunnery, but don't get on my nerves.

APACHE GIRL: Just what kind of shamelessness do you want?

HEADMASTER: (*To the Instructress.*) Did you explain in class what kind of shamelessness is required here?

INSTRUCTRESS: Good Lord, you know very well, Henrik Oskarovich, how devoted I am to my work!

HEADMASTER: I judge by results.

INSTRUCTRESS: (*To Apache Girl.*) Do the splits with more enthusiasm! You're nothing but a trouble-maker. (*The Apache Girl does it.*)

HEADMASTER: Yes, that's shameless, but it's obscene. You've got to do it so that the audience won't get upset. I seriously advise you to think about this, if you mean to devote yourself to art . . . Your shamelessness is rudimentary. On the other hand, if you're such a prude that people mustn't pull your hair and mustn't touch your waist, then crawl into a jar full of cotton, but don't study apache dancing. (*To the musicians, who are conversing loudly, playing cards on the piano keyboard.*) Are we disturbing you? (*They quiet down in embarrassment.*) This is a school, not a tavern! (*To the Apache Girl.*) What is an apache dance? An apache dance is when he beats her and she likes it, he pulls her by the hair and she smiles, he starts to strangle her and she falls in love. That's what an apache dance is. It's pure, unadulterated psychology. (*To the Apache.*) As for you, Comrade Merinov, there's nothing uninhibited about you.

APACHE: How so?

HEADMASTER: Here's what I mean. Make me an entrance like an uninhibited thug, but so that your lack of inhibitions comes across the footlights. (*The Apache makes an entrance as an uninhibited "thug."*) All right, now I'll show you what uninhibited means. (*He shows him smugly.*) You understand the difference? Did you understand that, Comrade Merinov? That's one. And two, you aren't enough of a thug, you aren't convincing.

APACHE: (*Offended.*) As for being uninhibited—that's as may be, but when it comes to being a thug, I not only know a lot of thugs, but in my own lifetime I broke 100 street-lights, ripped up the overcoat of a bourgeois like you with a knife, and I gave a certain lady ....

HEADMASTER: Yes, but it doesn't show when you dance. You're hiding your temperament somewhere.

APACHE: (*Exploding.*) You really want me to knock the socks off her?

HEADMASTER: That's a bit extreme.

APACHE: (*Seriously.*) I don't know about extreme or not extreme, but I'm telling you for the last time if you don't arrange for my debut in a theatre here this week I'm liable to do anything.—I ripped up the overcoat of a bourgeois like you with a knife,—got three months in stir.

HEADMASTER: Good Lord, Petr Ivanovich, you're behaving, excuse me please, like a child. I'm doing this on your behalf!

APACHE: This course costs twenty million!

HEADMASTER: Hmm! . . . What a hot-blooded fellow . . . Well, all right, let's do it your way. I don't hold grudges. You'll make your debut tomorrow, if the time is ripe. I have heaps of grateful testimonials. Music! . . . Let's begin. (*Frenzied "apache dance."*)

SERVANT: (*Running in.*) Gennady Potapovich is here.

(*The music breaks off. The Headmaster hurries left to meet the Manager of a music hall. The apaches go off right.*)

VARIETY MANAGER: (*A stout, shrewd publican, with pretentions to being a Western European.*) Am I late?

HEADMASTER: Of course not, for heaven's sake. Right on time.

MANAGER: Is the Baby Trio ready?

HEADMASTER: Not quite, Gennady Potapovich, they need more polish.

MANAGER: What are you doing to me, you cut-throat?! . . . I've got to have three acts for the finale.

HEADMASTER: Of course, if it's urgent . . . You did say that . . . (*To the Instructress.*) Klavdiya Ivanovna, detain the babies! Look lively! (*She flies backstage.*) Only be a little indulgent, because . . .

MANAGER: I'll be the way the audience is.

HEADMASTER: Day after tomorrow I'll have the apaches so ready for you, you'll smack your lips over them.

MANAGER: Give me a break, kiddo. I've already got some. Who needs 'em?

HEADMASTER: These're something extraordinary. (*In a whisper.*) You'll give me back that little I.O.U.! For heaven's sake, I'm making an effort!

MANAGER: We'll discuss that later. (*Points at Annushka.*) Who's that character?

HEADMASTER: A new girl.

MANAGER: Funny?

HEADMASTER: Haven't tried her out yet.

MANAGER: Don't be so shy! While the babykins are getting into their costumes, let's give her the once-over.

HEADMASTER: If you're interested . . . (*To Annushka.*) If you please, miss. (*She climbs up on stage. To the Manager.*) I'm actually rather glad you'll see what she is now and what I'll make of her in three months. (*To her.*) Show us what you can do!

ANNUSHKA: I sing, sir. But only just silly stuff, sort of like . . .

HEADMASTER: Whatever you want. (*To her.*) Now then! Don't be embarrassed! Mister Maestro will accompany you. Maestro, a few encouraging chords!

ANNUSHKA: (*Sings "Dear Little Cap" with piano accompaniment.*)

MANAGER: (*Jumps up in indescribable excitement.*) Now that's what I call brilliant! She's a world-class hit! Damn me if she ain't! She puts a lid on 'em all! Everyone of 'em! I was telling you I needed something in the gutsy line just now! . . . Something earthy, something that's got juice spontaneity! And here she is, here she is! Eureka, sir, eureka!

HEADMASTER: Not bad, but . . . she still has to study . . . acquire polish, so to speak . . .

MANAGER: To hell with polish! Nobody wants that nowadays.

You got no nose for what the public wants! Nowadays you need something that smells of sweat! That lets you feel the calluses on her hands! What's your name, my dear?

ANNUSHKA: Annushka.

MANAGER: Brilliant! A personal appearance by Annushka in her own repertoire! She's purer than Plevitskaya, my boy! How many imitators there'll be! My God! My head's spinning! Let's go to the office,—draw up a contract!

ANNUSHKA: (*Comes off the platform.*) I can't read or write, sir.

MANAGER: Nonsense!

HEADMASTER: Yes, but excuse me, Gennady Potapovich, what about me? After all she did come to my school!—And suddenly without a lesson . . . so . . . simply . . . where's the ethics in that? Where's the ethics?

MANAGER: In your I.O.U.! (*Gives it to him. To her.*) Let's go! . . . She doesn't even wear shoes! (*He leads her by the hand to the office, humming "Dear Little Cap." Appearing on the platform the Baby Trio watches them go in bewilderment, the same bewilderment as the Headmaster's, as he holds the I.O.U. in his hand, trying to figure out whether he has won or lost. Finally, the Headmaster recovers, puts the I.O.U. in his wallet and claps his hands.*)

HEADMASTER: From the top! Music!

BABY TRIO: (*Sings.*) "We got fed up fast with the cakewalk and the maxixe, and now there's a new dance, etc. . . . ''

CURTAIN

Popular Fiction
(*Van'kina Literatura*)
A Creative Process in One Act
1916
by

Boris Geyer

CHARACTERS:

He
She
The Writer
His Wife
The Writer's Friend
The Wife's Lady-Friend
The Cook
The Janitor

To one side of the stage, a small cozy nook, not unlike a boudoir, clearly separated from the rest of the stage. A low table with a lamp burning on it, next to a deep, soft armchair, in which He sits, a handsome young man dressed informally and holding a book. At his feet on a footstool, resting her head in his lap, She sits, a very young and beautiful woman in a peignoir. The greater part of the stage represents a shabby room with two doors: one to the kitchen and one to the bedroom, and two windows. Furnishings: a sparsely laid dining-table. As the curtain rises: He and She are in the nook; the Writer's Wife, a poorly dressed and unattractive middle-aged woman, and the crude, dirty cook, are in the room, setting the table. In the nook it is evening, in the room day. The two parts of the stage must not seem to be in the same apartment. The action is meant to take place in different towns at different times.

HE: So, chapter six today.

SHE: You know, whenever I hear you read this novel, I have such a longing to see the man who wrote it. I'm sure he must be good-looking. How beautiful, how fulfilling his life must be, what clear, what deep feelings he must have, how interesting the people around him must be. Sometimes I think, if I didn't love you so much, I would fall in love with him.

HE: You're getting carried away, my dear.

SHE: Are you jealous? Honestly, sometimes I have such a passionate longing to get just a glimpse of the life of the man who can create such a noble, beautiful work of art. After all, a writer is supposed to experience everything himself before he writes about it, isn't he? Isn't he?

HE: Of course . . . for the most part.

SHE: I envy him and the people around him.

HE: Ah, you're such an impressionable creature . . .

SHE: Darling . . . (*Kisses him.*) Are you angry?

HE: Don't be silly . . . Now, let's begin. (*Opens the book, but she prevents him by hugging and kissing him.*)

THE WRITER'S WIFE: Come on, stir your stumps, the master'll be home soon and calling for something to eat.

THE COOK: There's plenty of time. And I am hurryin'. (*Grumbles.*) The master, the master . . . He may be the guy in charge, but he's nobody's master. Wastes lots o' paper, but there ain't nothin' to eat . . . An aw-thor . . . Fooey! . . . (*Exits. Enter The Writer in an overcoat and hat, which he removes and throws on the sofa. He is a middle-aged man, poorly dressed, with a thick, dishevelled mane of hair.*)

THE WRITER: Oof, I've been running around like a dog in heat. I'm sweating like a pig.

WIFE: You get it?

WRITER: A measly twenty-five rubles. And with the inevitable proviso that they have chapter six tomorrow morning. Here, here's the money. (*Throws money on the table.*)

WIFE: We won't be able to pay the rent.

WRITER: Oh, to hell with the rent. I have to have chapter six by tomorow, and my head's as empty as a balloon. I don't know what I'm going to write.

WIFE: Have a bite to eat first.

WRITER: How the hell am I supposed to eat? Put something on

the desk. A glass of tea or something. We'll eat later. (*Goes over to the desk, takes a piece of paper, thinks for a minute and starts to write. The Cook brings in soup and goes out again. The wife eats.*)

HE: (*Kisses her.*) Enough of this fooling around, you little silly. Now listen. Chapter Six: "Roxanov, energetic and lively, cheered by the bonny spring sunshine, came beaming into the dining-room and the first thing that leapt to his eyes was—his Eugenia, even more beautiful and alluring than ever. 'My darling,' she greeted him in her melodious, silvery voice, holding out her beautiful, fragrant, tanned arms, bare to the elbow. 'You are just in time; the table awaits you.' Roxanov smiled at the sight of the snow-white table sparkling with silver and crystal and merrily said, 'No, my dearest. However much I would like to sit down with you, I cannot at this moment.' Eugenia capriciously pursed her beautiful crimson lips. 'We shall dine together,' he hastened to console her, 'but you know that I have a serious report to deliver tomorrow. On its success depends the fate of a thousand starving peasants: our younger brothers, Eugenia! Remember this and you will agree with me.' 'My darling, how noble you are,' whispered Eugenia, putting her soft fragrant arms around his neck and in her eyes glistened two round diamonds, two pure tears. He kissed her ardently and went into his simply but substantially furnished study.''

COOK: (*Enters with the roast.*) Master, that guy's here about that little matter. He says, when you gonna pay the rent? You owe a awful lot, he says, so the landlord's nervous.

WIFE: Oh, my God . . . Hm . . . I'm surprised he can't wait. Well, tell him we'll pay him tomorrow.

COOK: (*Goes out.*) Tomorrow, tomorrow. Nobody'll believe you, you derelick. (*Exits.*)

WRITER: And give him something to eat so he'll leave me in peace for a while. Damn the bastard. (*He writes.*)

HE: (*Reads.*) "The door opened softly and on the threshhold stood the pretty coquette of a parlor-maid, bowing respectfully. 'Master,' she said, 'the Nutrition Committee for the Poor Children has sent someone to see you . . .' 'Very good,' Roxanov interrupted her. 'I am very busy. Tell your mistress to give them thirty rubles and make my excuses. I am working on an urgent report.' The trim figure was heard to disappear behind the thick portière and Roxanov plunged back into his papers."

(*The Wife's Lady-Friend enters, a youngish, not-bad-looking-ish spinster.*)

LADY-FRIEND: Hello . . . Is Ivan Ivanovich at work again? Goodness, he's so hard-working.

WRITER: (*Through his teeth.*) Damn . . . Another interruption. (*Offstage a baby cries.*) Hello . . . (*He writes.*)

WIFE: Hello, sweetheart. I'm so glad you dropped in, otherwise a person could die of boredom. Well, what's new, Dunechka?

LADY-FRIEND: Oh, such a lot. Yesterday I saw some new material at the department store. Picture this—tiny little stripes and checks, and light blue polka dots running right through the middle. Polka dots, polka dots, and more polka dots. Like this. (*She demonstrates.*) A little check here, and a little stripe there, and a light blue polka dot there, and another polka dot. (*The Writer clutches his head.*)

WIFE: Oh, fascinating . . . I'll definitely stop by there tomorrow.

LADY-FRIEND: Be sure you go and have a look. And then at Madame Fifi's they're showing a new hat. An enormous ostrich plume along the side, a white one with the slightest yellow tinge, and in front . . . (*The baby's screams get louder.*)

WRITER: (*Throwing down his pen.*) Will you see to the baby! For Christ's sake . . . my head is splitting.

WIFE: Right away, right away . . . You didn't have to say anything. Marfushka can calm him down.

WRITER: You see to it—I've got work to do.

WIFE: Oh all right already . . . (*She goes out, slamming the door; the Writer writes.*)

HE: (*Reads.*) "A resonant, bird-like voice interrupted his thoughts. Before him stood Zoya, a friend of Eugenia's, and behind her he could discern his wife's laughing face. 'Goodness,' Zoya teased, wagging her finger slyly as her charming little mouth flashed two rows of pearly teeth. 'Can anyone work so much?' 'What am I to do?,' Roxanov leaned wearily over the back of his chair and happily squeezed Zoya's slender, warm fingers. 'It is our duty. But for your sake I am glad to take a bit of a break.' Roxanov loved this intelligent, educated girl, and something vague but sweet, a gnawing feeling irrepressibly crept over him. 'You know, Eugenia,' said Zoya in her deep, velvety voice, 'you know, in my last paper I won a glorious victory in defense of women's rights.' 'You are a clever creature,' replied Eugenia and suddenly her face took on a look of anxious attention. She put a rosy fingertip with its tiny, pointed nail to her lips and saying anxiously, 'Our little baby is crying,' quietly slipped out of the room. They were alone together.''

LADY-FRIEND: (*Stands beside the Writer and flirts.*) How angry you are. You drove your wife out.

WRITER: Please understand, I've got a chapter to do.

LADY-FRIEND: How silly. You are so ingenious, you writers, it's just wonderful. You're writing about love, I suppose?

WRITER: I'm writing about you.

LADY-FRIEND: Tee hee . . . May I look? (*Bends over.*) For shame, what a scrawl. I can't make it out. You should get a typewriter . . . But look, what lovely new material my blouse is made of. (*Bends over very near to him.*)

WRITER: Hm . . . You're a chubby one, aren't you . . . Heh heh . . .

LADY-FRIEND: Oh, what are you . . .

WRITER: We're poets, liberated types, we love women, damn it . . . Since you were talking about material . . . Hm . . . hm . . . (*Tries to embrace her. The sound of a baby crying and a door slamming close by.*) Damn, here comes the gargoyle. (*Leaves her and writes.*)

HE: (*Reads.*) ''Zoya drew near to Roxanov and placed a thick manuscript before him. 'Look, this is my new work on the woman question.' And suddenly a kind of wave, quite like a mist, came over Roxanov, so that his mind went dead, his whole body seemed to coil into a spring and he felt that an inexorable power was forcing him that very moment to hold that wonderful girl in an embrace, to press her to him passionately, to cover her with frantic kisses . . . Her beauty was quite different from Eugenia's beauty. A young, lissome body . . . He felt the power of passion and the innocence of his caresses. And suddenly the faint weeping of a baby could be heard . . . His baby . . . He winced nervously and said in a shrill voice: 'Good' and turned away. He was ashamed.''

LADY-FRIEND: (*Near the Writer.*) Ooh you fraidy-cat . . . (*The Wife enters. The Lady-friend quickly moves away. The Wife looks at her suspiciously.*) Did you pacify your loud-screamer?

WIFE: (*Drily.*) I pacified him.

LADY-FRIEND: Hm . . . So you'll go to Madame Fifi's? See that hat, it's simply marvelous, that's what it is. An ostrich plume on the side, and a round ribbon-bow in front. A funny kind of ribbon-bow with a greenish tinge.

WIFE: Fine, fine.

LADY-FRIEND: What are you so sour about?

WIFE: No reason . . .

LADY-FRIEND: This is odd, I must say. I pay her a visit and she . . .

WIFE: A visit so you can flirt with other people's husbands . . . we know your kind.

LADY-FRIEND: How do you mean? . . . What's that supposed to mean? . . . To insult a respectable girl all of a sudden with remarks like that? . . . It's practically rude, I must say.

WIFE: You'd better keep your mouth shut, you brazen hussy.

WRITER: What's come over you, love?

WIFE: Shut up . . . You'd better bite your tongue.

LADY-FRIEND: I never expected such a reprimand. All right then. I don't want to know you any more. Spit on you if that's the way you want it . . . Fooey! (*Exits.*)

WIFE: Spit on yourself, honey. (*Walks quickly around the room; the Writer writes.*)

HE: (*Reads.*) "Eugenia, entering the room and glancing at them both, suddenly turned pale. The atmosphere was quite saturated with something monstrously heady and thousands of voices screamed in her ears, affecting her horribly. "What's wrong, Zoya darling?,' she whispered, almost choking, not knowing what to say. Zoya glanced at her with a pure, innocent, rock-crystalline gaze, and suddenly she too experienced a kind of shudder. She hurriedly began to make her farewells. Eugenia embraced her tightly and, with a barely perceptible quaver in her voice, said 'You still don't understand anything, my precious child.' "

WIFE: What's all this? You planning to have affairs?

WRITER: What affairs?

WIFE: What was she doing, right on top of your desk?

WRITER: Who the hell knows? She was jabbering and keeping me from working, the idiotic chatterbox.

WIFE: Is that right . . . When I'm here she's a chatterbox, but when

I'm in the other room this chatterbox is probably a sweetie and a dear and a beautiful . . .

WRITER: What's come over you, my love?

WIFE: I know you. Any frilly skirt comes along, you start drooling, all set to run after her. All men are trash.

WRITER: And you're a fool . . . Imagining who the hell knows what, and screaming.

WIFE: I'm a fool. You're a blockhead yourself and a good-for-nothing into the bargain. Carries on hanky-panky in his own home and then dares to say . . . Pooh . . .

WRITER: Stop screaming . . . Remember who you are and who I am. I took you out of the gutter.

WIFE: You what? Who squandered away my dowry? Who cheated my mother and father? Ah, you bastard . . . Son-of-a-bitch . . . no-talent hack . . .

WRITER: (*Putting his hands over his ears.*) Let me work . . . The devil tied me to this female . . . Beat it!

WIFE: (*Throws a plate at him and sits sobbing on the sofa.*) Miserable trash . . . Monster . . . (*The Writer writes.*)

HE: (*Reads.*) " 'I know everything,' Eugenia said and fell helplessly on the sofa. Roxanov stood up and asked in confusion, 'What everything?' 'You are deceiving me.' 'I swear to you by all that's holy to me, it isn't so.' She sat there still, pale and wan . . . immobile . . . Their conversation was brief. There were no tears or hysterical screams. She was sad, but stubbornly insisted on having it her way, he indignantly offered arguments and proof. 'It's not for me to rebuke you,' she said, wearily rising from the sofa. 'We have given one another everything we could. Now it's over.' 'My dearest,' he exclaimed, holding his arms out to her, but she softly and silently turned and went. In the doorway she threw him a glance, and it struck Roxanov as something threatening and fatal.''

THE WRITER'S FRIEND: (*A scatterbrain with sweeping movements. Enters and speaks in stentorian tones.*) Vanka! . . . drudging away? That lousy scribbling . . . I knew it . . . Mariya Ivanovna, my abject greetings.

WIFE: Hello.

FRIEND: (*Greets the writer.*) Why so gloomy, nose to the grindstone? Obviously you haven't had a drink lately, right?

WRITER: Damn you both . . . I've got a carload of scribbling to do, pal.

FRIEND: Stop writing this garbage, it don't mean anything, it's all lies. Let's have a drink.

WRITER: All right, we'll have a bite, I'm not against it. Only pardon me, pal, if I go on working.

FRIEND: You gotta get some color in that nose, damn it . . . I'm going to flirt with Mariya Ivanovna here.

WIFE: Yes, yes. We should punish him soundly.

FRIEND: Right you are. (*Takes snacks and vodka from the table and pours a drink.*) All right, we'll carry on on our own . . . (*They drink.*)

WRITER: It won't get in the way of my inspiration.

FRIEND: Passion's the ticket. Give it to 'em with hot pepper sauce. Readers love it so long as it's romantic. Nightingales, the moon, the scent of the roses and the rustle of silk skirts. And all for five kopeks. They're pretty stingy laying out money for books. Now if it's a picture, especially if it's a smutty one, that's another story, but paying for something serious—you're out of luck, pal.

WRITER: That's not quite . . .

FRIEND: Skip it, don't try to convince me . . . Once upon a time maybe, but not any more. Now it's feed the face. But you hold the banner high, churn out counts and dukes . . . and with hot pepper sauce so that . . . Well, down the hatch with this dishwater. (*They drink.*)

WRITER: The worst part is they've started to pay less. Used to be seven kopeks a line, now it's five.

FRIEND: Spit on 'em . . . You get more passion with an undressing scene. A real writer should wave the petticoats high . . . I mean, his banner, the ensign itself . . . Drink up, kiddo, don't be ashamed. (*They drink; the Writer writes. The Friend goes over to the Wife and sits beside her on the sofa.*)

HE: (*Reads.*) "Roxanov stood in a stupor. Her glance had seemed to pierce him. 'What is this? What is this?' he whispered with paling lips. He was so rapt in thought that he failed to notice that his friend Marinsky had come in. He was a perfect gentleman from head to foot. His elegant manners, graceful restrained gestures, refined speech always acted on Roxanov in the most soothing manner and his arrival immediately had a pleasant effect on him. 'You're depressed,' Marinsky noted, with a gentle smile. Roxanov refrained from relating to his friend what had just occurred. Soon a bottle of champagne stood before them, and both men sipped it mildly, slowly; Roxanov felt that serenity had returned to him once more. 'You have a sacred obligation,' Marinsky said with profound conviction. 'Hold high your banner . . . the service of society, ordained from on high, aspiration towards the ideal, such is your mission . . . Show people the right path and they will understand and appreciate you.' And this quiet restrained voice gently resounded in the thickening gloom and inspired hope and faith in a bright and better future.''

FRIEND: So, worthiest of ladies, Mariya Ivanovna. You say Vanka's been misbehaving, has he?

WIFE: The bastard isn't worth talking about.

FRIEND: But you'll teach him a fine lesson, the cad.

WIFE: He's ready to chase after every skirt.

FRIEND: Ah, super-villain . . .

WIFE: Yes . . . in his own home too.

WRITER: Lies, lies . . .

FRIEND: Scribble, don't eavesdrop . . . Mariya Ivanovna, you should take revenge on him . . . that's the best thing to do. Come on, I'll make love to you.

WIFE: Oh, what are you on about . . .

FRIEND: I can lay on Spanish passion . . . Love with castanets and a guitar under my cloak.

WRITER: Try it, try it! I'll thank you for it.

FRIEND: Let's give it a try . . . All right Mariya Ivanovna, shall I declare my love to you to the strains of a fandango? Do you know ''The Guadalquivir roars and rushes'' and ''through the iron railings a wondrous knife was stuck.''

WIFE: (*Laughing affectedly.*) You're a pretty weird caballero . . .

HE: (*Reads.*) ''Marinsky soon took his leave. Roxanov stood up and slowly went to Eugenia's room. She attracted him, alluring, beautifully seductive, and he thought of how he would dispel her suspicions, how she would laugh her pearly laugh. And her downy cheek, like a peach, would cling to his lips. At her door he heard voices. All at once he recognized them. 'I love you,' Marinsky sighed in his melodious baritone . . . Roxanov recoiled, wanted to fling the door open, but his innate nobility came to the fore. It was vile to eavesdrop—he whispered and without awaiting Eugenia's reply, recovering himself he returned to his study.''

WIFE: You can start now. I'm going for a walk, and you can escort me.

FRIEND: With you to the ends of the earth. Listen, Scribbler Petrovich . . . Mariya Ivanovna and I have decided to go for a stroll.

WRITER: (*Noticeably drunk.*) Well, clear out then . . .

WIFE: I'm going to look at that hat . . .

WRITER: Look at the devil for all I care . . .

WIFE: Vulgar creature . . .

FRIEND: On our way then . . . (*Speaking abrubtly and drinking.*) Goodbye, Novelist Angryvich . . .

WRITER: Actually, I'm tipsy . . . or all but. Well then, I'll compensate by making a scene right now. Ugh . . . (*The Wife and Friend leave. The Writer writes.*)

HE: (*Reads.*) ''In the luxurious study a feeble groan rang out. He did not believe, would not believe, and wrung his slender aristocratic hands in despair. 'She turned him down, she sent him away,' he consoled himself, but jealousy, like an infuriate beast, rent his bared heart. The maid came in, pale and perplexed. She was holding a small pink envelope, which she handed to him. With trembling hands Roxanov tore it open and reeled back. There it was, the awful truth. His wife . . . The lines leaped to his eyes, twisted, sneered and chuckled in savage voices. 'I am leaving you, Marinsky is going with me: Do not wait and do not write. Eugenia.' Him . . . With him? . . . With Marinsky . . . With his best friend? . . . With his mainstay, the man whom he trusted so? . . . What a blow . . . What a blow . . . 'Ha ha,' Roxanov began to roar with laughter. 'There it is. There's faith in mankind, in ideals . . . There's your answer . . .' ''

SHE: Did you notice how passionately, with what élan that scene was written? How deeply it must have thrilled its author . . .

COOK: (*Enters.*) That there janitor's back agin. Come about the rent, I shouldn't wonder.

WRITER: The janitor? . . . Throw him out . . .

COOK: No way . . . Gotta see you and nobody else.

WRITER: To hell with him . . . All right, show him in . . .

COOK: Sure thing. (*Exits. Enter the Janitor.*)

JANITOR: 'Scuse me, sir . . .

WRITER: Well?

JANITOR: It's like this, this here landlord, like, 's real angry like.

WRITER: Just deliver the message.

JANITOR: It's like this, see . . . The landlord, he says like you ain't paid for three months, like get out, he says, you're out on your neck . . .

WRITER: All right, all right, take it easy . . .

JANITOR: You had it. We're jest plain folks, but lemme add, like there ain't no other way.

WRITER: But I'll pay him tomorrow. Or, the day after tomorrow.

JANITOR: You had it . . . We're jest or'nery folks, but the landlord says if there ain't no money tomorrow, out, he says out on their necks.

WRITER: Hm. (*Fumbles in his pockets and gives him a tip.*) There, my man, take this in case I overstay my welcome another two days, got me?

JANITOR: That's not like impossible. It's all right by me, but the landlord says if you don't pay tomorrow . . .

WRITER: Not one day's grace?

JANITOR: S'far's I'm concerned, help y'self, we're jest or'nery folks, but . . .

WRITER: Then clear the hell out of here . . . Get out before I murder you . . .

JANITOR: (*Moves backwards.*) We're jest plain folks, so tomorrow please . . . (*Exits.*)

WRITER: (*Clutches his head.*) Aaah . . . Tomorrow? . . . Would you mind? And I've still got this novel . . . And my head's in a fog from this vodka. How 'bout that janitor, huh? A regular devil . . . Shoulda took him and thrown him out . . . Foo-oo . . . (*Sits and writes.*)

HE: (*Reads.*) "In the corner before him a misty spot began to grow . . . It towered up and expanded, and suddenly Roxanov recognized it for what it was. The thing which always, at all times, had hindered him in every way, the curse of his life, his *memento mori*. It stood before him crude, sneering, a personification of the dark powers, brute force and savage abuse. And a coarse, heavy voice rang in his ears . . . like the sound of a great cracked bell . . . 'You will create nothing. Roxanov, your efforts for the good of your oppressed fellow-man I shall destroy—I am all powerful. Your struggle for your neighbor's happiness I shall crush in my iron fist. Your wife, whom you loved selflessly, has run away from you. Your friend has deceived you; you thought you were strong but you were mistaken. You are as impotent as you ever were, and as it was so it shall be—I will be here tomorrow and every day. And you . . . perhaps tomorrow you will not be. I am the all-powerful master of your fate.' Roxanov strained towards the figure, but it had already dissolved into thin air and a dismal empty corner stared him in the face.''

SHE: (*Excited.*) It's a symbol; that's so good . . . So good . . . It's the dark power that stifles everything bright, everything idealistic. I understand, I understand . . .

WRITER: Well, just a couple of lines to go and then it's done . . . But that damned janitor! What am I going to do tomorrow? . . . Such is the fate of us writers. (*Declaims.*) ''Fellow writers, there is something fatal in your destiny.'' . . . Oh well, tomorrow's tomorrow—and then we'll see, but today we'll plug painfully away at what needs to be done . . . (*Drains the glass in one swig and writes for a while, then bends over the table and falls asleep.*)

HE: (*Reads.*) ''Roxanov put a trembling cold hand to his burning brow. 'It's all over,' he whispered, 'all over. Wait for tomorrow? Wait to recover your strength? No . . . Even there you are no longer in control . . .' And laughing wildly, he slowly walked over to the desk and picked up a dagger. Turning it over in his hands, he thoughtfully cast it aside, then quickly pulled out of his pocket a packet of poison, poured it into the bottle of champagne and drained it at one draught. Big green, yellow, and red dots swam before his eyes, he stood erect, then mechanically dropped into an armchair and his head fell noiselessly onto the desk. Roxanov was dead.''

SHE: Dead . . . dead . . . What a pity! Oh! I'm so sorry . . . His dreams were shattered, his ideals were shattered! Everything beautiful, everything holy. And he had to live through all of it . . .

HE: Who, my dear?

SHE: The writer! I know! I feel it. Oh! how I'd like to see the noble man who's been through so much suffering. Just one little look . . . just to offer him a word of comfort . . .

WRITER: (*Mutters in his sleep.*) Damned polka dots . . .

SHE: Poor man! poor man! . . . He's dead! he died all alone . . . (*Weeps in He's lap. The Writer snores. The snoring and the weeping blend for a few moments.*)

CURTAIN

At the Cine-Mato-Scopo-Bio-Phono—etc.-Graph
(V kine-mato-skopo-bio-fono i proch.-graf)
1910
by
Nadezhda Teffi

MANAGER: Please, Mister Explainer, don't mix up the slides again, the way you did last time.

NARRATOR: What do you mean, last time? I don't understand.

MANAGER: Like when the screen showed the Kaiser and a battleship being launched, you were blah-blahing about natural history and some kind of butterfly pollen. That sort of thing can have a bad effect, not to mention I don't like paying money for nothing. You've got a lovely voice, I don't deny it, and you know your stuff just great, but now and then you ought to look at the screen.

NARRATOR: I don't like to stand with my back to the audience. It's the fault of that nitwit projectionist—talk to him.

PROJECTOR: (*Starting to hiss.*) Ddzz . . .

NARRATOR: (*Clears his throat and, his back to the screen, turns his inspired face directly into the light.*) Gracious ladies and gentlemen! Before you is the most venerable river in South America, the Amazon, so-called because of the passion of the beautiful ladies of the region for horseback riding. The Amazon's magnificent waves roll on day and night, forming waterfalls, springs, and tributaries, beneath whose splashing all sorts of different things take place. Bushes, trees, sand, and other varieties of nature border its picturesque banks. Now another view . . . for look, we stand amid the gloomy ruins of the Coliseum. Horror grips our limbs and rivets our attention. Here a mighty tyrant gave proof of his hard-heartedness. (*Hm . . . change it, what's wrong, don't take forever!* . . .) Well now, as if by the wave of a magic wand, we are transported to ancient Greece and stand before the statue of holy Aphrodite, who has been astounding many ages with the grace of her bearing. (*Well?*) And here is the most respected city of Venice, exceeding in its beauties the fancies of the most experienced imagination.

PROJECTOR: Dzzz . . .

NARRATOR: (*Huh? Stop! I know, I know.*) Now we shall beat a temporary retreat to the realm of natural history. Before you is an image to be observed with the aid of the super-microscope, the pride of the twentieth century. It shows the tiniest anatomies, invisible to the naked eye, a bed-bug the size of an elephant and an infusoria in a piece of cheese. Many things are essential in nature, and people, all unawares, carry whole worlds beneath the nails of each of their fingers.

Now we shall take a peep at Vesuvius. What can be more magnificent than this erupting picture of na . . . (*What? But —that's not my business! I'm sorry. But I didn't mix up the slides. Go to the next one! The next one! Oh hell!*) Before you, gracious ladies and gentlemen, is a rare example of a viviparous fish. Nature in her lavish vari. . . (*Why Vesuvius when I've gone to fish? Hold on to that one at least. It was straight! I'll straighten you!*) Smoke curls from the grandiose, funnel-shaped crater that picturesquely stands etched against the azure blue of the southern sky. Yet another wave of the magic wand (*How long will you be dawdling?*) . . . and look, we are on the shores of Naples, the most wonderful city in the world. Right, a thousand times right is the proverb (*Don't interrupt!*) that says: "He who has not drunk the waters of Naples, has drunk nothing." (*What? A fossil? Who told you to do that? Change the slide or else!*) Before us is Pygmalion, who by means of his own inspiration brought to life (*What's the pig doing there? Why a pig? You're always fumbling in the wrong box! Get rid of it!*) Hmm . . . a marvelous marble statue, which he sculpted with his own hands (*Again! Didn't I just tell you to get rid of it! You think if you show a pig with its tail in front that's Pygmalion.*) out of the most delicate marble. Many are the wonders of nature, but the wonders of art are no slackers for all that.

PROJECTOR: Dzzz . . .

NARRATOR: And there, another image of the wonderful creativity of anonymous hands—the Venus de Milo, lauded by all. Ranked for her beauty in the assembly of the gods, she nevertheless displays shame (*What did I just say . . . why straighten it! You should remove it right now and get rid of it. There's no reason for the pig when I'm talking about a different slide!*), which shows modesty, characteristic of ancient Greeks even on the highest rungs of the social ladd. . . (*You go on and do what you want! You're the cross I bear!*) ladder. And now another moment . . . from this group from an unknown chisel we turn to the boundless steppe of our great and awesome count . . . (*If you intend to show your pig twenty times in a row, we'd better take an intermission, because the audience may want its money back. Everyone has paid and has the right to ask for a refund. I tell you you'd better put out the lamp. What? Who is the manager going to chew out!*) And now, gracious ladies and gentlemen, we shall take a ten-minute break, after which we shall once more set out on our far-flung journey over the whole world, so broadening to the intellectual faculties and spiritual side of our nature, even though we improve them sitting in our comfortable seats. (*Nitwit! You, you're a nitwit!*) And so, farewell to the isle of the Celebes with its local customs and striking environments.

Baliev and the "Bat"

(Vecher v "Letuchke")

1969

by

V. Levshin

The auditorium was small, but had a balcony and a box near the stage. However, this box was occupied by the "musical component"—a lady pianist and two or three instrumentalists headed by the invariable conductor and composer of almost all the music played here, A. Arkhangelsky. A green velvet curtain with appliqués—a garland of flowers and two histrionic masks with open mouths, somewhat reminiscent of Baliev . . .

N. F. Baliev appears at the proscenium. Applause. Baliev does not react to it, he holds the folds of the curtain behind his back and attentively looks round the hall, the enormous whites of his eyes glittering. Someone has come late and is hurrying to his seat in the third row, but the place is already filled by someone with a complimentary ticket. The comp-holder, stepping on his neighbors' feet, moves out of the row. That's all Baliev needs. He sees off the unlucky fellow with a malicious smile and remarks, as if by the way: "Now there's a man who stands out from the crowd." The man gets embarrassed and disappears into the aisle. Someone boldly tries to heckle Baliev. Nikita Fyodorovich ripostes no less boldly: "Repeat that, I didn't catch it. You won't die of hunger, you've got a mouthful of porridge." Naturally, there is no repetition.

The first number in the program. Usually this is a dramatic, even a melodramatic sketch. Either "The Cathedral of Constance" from the poem by A. Maykov with superb medieval stained-glass windows, beneath which the trial of Jan Hus is played out. Or

"Cleopatra and the Crocodile" in which you are transported to ancient Egypt. Today it's a scene from Gorky's fairy tale "The Mother," in which Podgorny plays the cruel tyrant Timur. It is all performed seriously and at the same time very lightly, elegantly. The scenery very exactly represents the necessary period, and yet remains purely theatrical. And even though the actors are playing strong emotions, you still get the sense that this is a performance.

And now we move to a frivolous genre: Madeleine Bouché! The second, invariably the second number of the program. Before the closed curtains steps a charming young actress. A sort of peasant lass, but one who hails from Brittany—peaches and cream! A dazzling smile, bare arms, hands on hips.

Madeleine Bouché sings French ditties, sometimes in translation, sometimes in the original, with excellent French pronunciation. It is impossible to describe her charm, musicality, a wonderful laugh that conveys both innocence and temperament. Almost all her ditties have meaningless refrains. For instance: "The sailors of Bordeaux tra-la and even of Rochelle haul the fishies on board and merrily sing: tra-la, tra-la, tra-la, tra-la, tra-la, tra-la, tra-la!" The ditties are extremely simple-minded, many of them even vulgar. Her hit song is "The Hunter." I remember it because it is always played to me. I involuntarily represent the hunter himself whom the singer is addressing. Madeleine Bouché, and Nikita Fyodorovich after her now coax me, now wag a finger at me, now pity me, and at the end send me an airy kiss. No matter what the song, the applause is tumultuous. But Baliev has already imperceptibly made a hurried escape, in order to re-enter in time.

"Papa the Brigand, or The Sorely Beaten Victim of a Misalliance!" he announces.

On stage is a drawing-room in an eighteenth-century mansion. Everything is white and gold: clavier, armchairs, little étagères with clocks . . . At the clavier in panniers and a white powdered wig is the daughter of the house. Beside her, her suitor (with fascinating dimples on his cheeks!) in a silk camisole and snow-white jabot. But this refined couple sings its duet underlining all the ohs . . .

Then there's a love scene. The servant Parashka appears in a sarafan . . . and addresses the suitor:

> When he heard you've paid a call
> Our master 'gan to caterwaul.

Parashka reveals the master's idea: he will disguise himself as a brigand or bandit, frighten away the suitor and chase him out of the house . . . The farce ends with a general reconciliation and more verses . . .

The show goes on. Baliev again comes before the curtain. Note that any pause that might dampen the ardor of the spectator is out of the question at the "Bat." Tempo, tempo!

Baliev announces:

' "Three young soldiers went to war"—a song of Yvette Guilbert. Yvette Guilbert is so famous that you have only to open a volume of the encyclopedia at the letter G and you . . . won't find anything about her." '

On stage is a cloth backdrop and two stylized windows: the king stares out of one, and the queen out of the other. That's how it always is at the "Bat": one scene scrupulously preserves the style of the period, the next takes on a deliberately conventionalized form.

Each verse of the song consists of one line, repeated twice, following by the same refrain: "Ra-ta-plan!"—percussive as a drum beat. Three English soldiers enter to the march, led by the drummer-boy-Kolumbova, who sings:

Three young soldiers went to war.
Ra-ta-plan!
A rose shown red in the first one's hat.
The king's daughter at the casement sat . . .

No sooner has the curtain closed . . . then Baliev stands before it, and, knitting his brows, gloomily stares at the audience. Now they are applauding him—so much serious comedy in his face, reminiscent of a full moon.

The curtain parts. On stage is a room at court in the time of Napoleon Bonaparte. Everything in the style of the period. The Emperor and Josephine are carrying on a high-toned dialogue, nothing suggests a scandal. But then an adjutant appears. Napoleon asks: is the car ready? The adjutant is embarrassed, he reports: no, it isn't, the chauffeur is missing. The Emperor is impatient, he demands . . . He isn't allowed to finish his sentence. A remark sharply rings out in the auditorium.

"Rubbish! There were no automobiles at the time of Napoleon!"

A second's confusion, and the show goes on. But the remark from the house is repeated more insistently. Napoleon shuts up in dismay. In the audience shouts and hissing erupt: "Throw out the hooligan!" But the "hooligan" continues to have it his own way. Baliev comes on stage and asks the audience to calm down.

The play goes on from the moment when the adjutant appeared. But the scandal in the audience rages with new force: "There were no automobiles!," "Hooligan," "Rubbish!," "We paid our money!," "There weren't any!"

Napoleon tears off his wig and shouts hysterically: "I cannot act in these conditions." A battle in the audience. Baliev intercedes between spectators and actors. Finally the curtain closes. Nikita Fyodorovich is depressed, announces an intermission, during which the audience buzzes like a stirred-up beehive, so masterfully, so do-it-yourselfishly has this practical joke been pulled off! . . .

During this intermission, let us consider what, ultimately, does Baliev himself contribute to the performance?

People usually say, "You go to 'The Bat' and you hear a cascade of Baliev's witticisms." An impression is created that all night long Baliev does nothing but make jokes. A troublesome error! Baliev rarely makes jokes, and only when he is parrying hecklers in the audience. Not only does he not flabbergast the audience with a torrent of jokes, on the contrary, he is for the most part sparing of words. And if his jokes are current throughout the city, that is principally because they are infrequent, but well-aimed. This notion of Baliev's loquacity proceeds from the fact that he is before the public's eyes all night, takes part (almost silently!) in all the acts, and behaves in a relaxed manner, like a cheerful host, welcoming his dear guests. True, only so long as those guests don't behave like boors. His silence is so eloquent that a few words produce the effect of a long monologue. Baliev seldom repeats his jokes. But even when he does repeat them he finds a way out.

"The wittiest man in the world," he replies to the charge, "is Jerome K. Jerome; and he thought nothing was wittier than to repeat his name." Nikita Fyodorovich doesn't put on his own act every night. And then it's only songs. Strictly speaking, it isn't singing but an idiosyncratic melo-declamation.

Baliev's unusual charm, his inimitable and unusual repertory of smiles (from benevolent to sarcastic), his scowling eyebrows, his round face looking out from behind the curtain,—all this creates an impression that he is conversing with you non-stop, that the entire evening revolves around him, whereas in fact he is very modest, tries to be in the shadow during the acts, doesn't meddle but helps the performers. That is why all the participants in the show have such wonderful memories of Baliev.

A Visit to The Stray Dog, St. Petersburg

(from *Le Plan de l'aiguille*)

1927

by

Blaise Cendrars

"Hello. What are you doing here?"

"May I come in and make a phone-call?"

"Come in then. Watch out, there's a step."

The door to The Stray Dog opens. Pronin stands back to let Dan Yack get by. There aren't many people in the cabaret. A pile of furs on one table and a flotilla of galoshes. Some women in the seats. Few men and everyone sprawled on the ground. The smoke in the place blinds you with astigmatism. Sight becomes troubled, uncertain. The figures on stage move in the distance and then suddenly loom closer and seem as distorted as in an aquarium. Strange tropical fish rise from the depths, crawl along the walls to grow iridescent beneath the vitrified border-lights of the ceiling. They are luminous paintings by Yakovlev, Sudeikin, Grigoriev. The heat trickles down like cosmetics and a little light bulb floats at the bottom of each glass on a little buoy of lemon peel. Like Indian pearl-divers in Lake Titicaca, people breathe with the aid of two straws. They are all crouched in a vase of magenta velvet and polar bear skins. Little globules of ether and soda pop against their cheeks. Their eyes blink. All the faces are crinkled, cracked, and sizzle like a drop of opium at the tip of a needle. There are whipped-cream women whose mouth, if you can see their mouth, is like a preserved fruit, purplish; others foam like champagne or lint. Their laughter makes you sick to your stomach and, as it rises up your leg, you have to fight back seasickness. Pitching and nausea. Lovely Olechka and that filthy little Kiki capsize, tickled. The trays whirl, bringing still more glasses upon glasses and rippling bottles. The waitresses, moving like silent algae, are dressed in tight short pants of coarse green silk-corduroy. Each one is wearing a Veronese-green wig. Pronin alone has one of parrot blue. Teffi is the one on stage right now. What her black gown with its long train doesn't cover—her breasts, the ganglia of her neck, her face fit to be slapped, her puckered-up phiz, her poached eyes,—looks like a bulb of garlic. She is singing the fashionable verse: *Polire! Lustrare!*

> *Quando fummo sulle scale, piccol' moll',*
> *La mi prese il cazzo in mano, piccol' moll',*
> *La mi disse, Capitano*
> *Sali! Sali!*
> *Sali, sali, sali, sali, sali, sul sofà piccol' moll'.*

Her success is her unadorned voice which diffuses the sacrosanct Neapolitan odor.

> *Polire! Lustrare!*

Dan Yack merely walks across the club, stopping his nose as if he were crossing a fish market open to the noonday sun, a marketplace full of garbage, refuse, swarms of flies, cheese stench, gutted fish, rotted melons, puddles of bleach, and takes refuge in the telephone booth, not without having, in his haste, slipped on some filthy fruit peel and almost sprawled full-length on a horrible creel of nocturnal vice, full as a carrion with its four shoes in the air, exposed to the glare of three spotlights as it plays the two-backed beast. His precipitant retreat unleashes a wild laugh, and glasses and bottles burst into shivers. Through the padded door, he hears the delirious hall howl his name to the tune of *Anglichan'e molodets* . . . (Attaboy, Englishman . . .) His eyes stray to the obscene water-colors of Elena Petrovna which upholster the walls of the booth. That woman spread-eagled beneath four bent banana trees, each limb solidly attached to a stalk, while a mad elephant rapes her with his trunk. Those nude gentlemen, monocle in place, each with the same tattoo on his right breast, making a daisy-chain, spiralling on the mother-of-pearl beach of an atoll. That adolescent swooning as he is sucked by a starfish in a landscape of madrepores. Those three early-rising young girls, emerging from the sea, co-penetrated, united, tied, entwined by a long blind serpent which wriggles through all their natural orifices, making them squirm, grimace, laugh. Those fish, those sexuate birds; those lewd and transparent animals, tragic and human; those greedy plants, those flowers bearing the pistils and pustules of sin; that hermaphroditic antelope sniffing cocaine and those innocent giraffes browsing on ampules of morphine; that ape crushing a phallus between two stones to devour the kernel, while his mate whose ass is sewn up is trying to undo the catch so she can have fun with the banana she holds in her paw.

Scene-curtain and center aisle in the auditorium of the Bat, Moscow.

Sketch of the Café Momus in Warsaw.

*Nikolay Evreinov in drag as
a music hall chanteuse.*

*Three faces of Nikita Baliev.
Upper left, "Skimpy box-office!"
Upper right, "Sold Out." Below,
"What?! An advance?!!"*

*The skopka or Nativity puppet-
play at the Green Balloon, 1911.
The figure in the middle is
Teofil Trzciński.*

IV

THE AVANT-GARDE CABARET
NEOPATHETISM, FUTURISM, AND DADA

1910-1920

A PROGRAMMATIC APPROACH TO THE CABARET AS A MEDIUM OF avant-garde art was advanced by the Neopathetic Cabaret, an expansion of literary evenings held since 1909 by the proto-expressionist New Club. These readings took place in various Berlin locales and were led by the twenty-five-year-old law student Kurt Hiller. Hiller formulated a Nietzschean aesthetic profile for the cabaret, in opposition to the "art for art's sake," mystical literary approach of Rilke, Hofmannsthal, and Stefan George. He called for a new type of poet, the "literary politician." As Hiller stated in "The Cabaret and the Brain—Hail," his opening address on 6 July 1910: "Fervor not as the formalistic gesticulation of suffering sons of prophets, but as universal merriment, as panic laughter. So it must be understood that we do not all think it undignified and ignoble to interject the most serious philosopheme into music hall songs and (cerebral) silliness; on the contrary: precisely because philosophy has a vital, not an academic, meaning for us, and is not a field of study, a business, a mortality or a burst of sweat, but experience, we find it much more appropriate to a cabaret than to a lecture platform or a quarterly journal."

These "adventures of the mind" were both literary and musical: Wedekind's verse was recited by the actress Tilla Durieux; Else Lasker-Schüller, "the Black Swan of Israel," read her cabbalistic poems; shadow-plays were staged; and pianists played Debussy and Schoenberg. One of the outstanding talents of the Neopathetics was Dr. Salomo Friedländer (1871-1946), who, under the name Mynona, read his grotesque anecdotes and tales. Mynona saw himself as the "exterminator of the soul's vermin," though one member described him as "a kind of boy-hustler of the intellect."

Hiller broke with the Neopathetics in 1911 and opened the Gnu at the Café Austria, devoted to the "Deabsurdification and Debarbarization of Humanity." The Neopathetics held their final session the next year, after their new leader, Georg Heym, drowned in a skating accident.

A Violent Pastime
(Der gewaltige Zeitvertrieb)
An Objective Sketch
by
Mynona (Dr. Salomo Friedländer)

An old man was sitting on a cloud and thundering. A wanderer through heaven came by and stopped for a moment in surprise. "What are you doing there?"—The old man was about to give a surly and rude reply when, for once, a good-natured mood came over him; his wrinkled face crumpling into cordial folds, he cast a friendly glance at the pilgrim from beneath his bushy gray brows and said with incredible simplicity, "I'm thundering." "Yes, but don't you get bored with it?" "God forbid," said the old man, while he kept on thundering, "just you take a look down yonder." The pilgrim looked down and saw a house in a field catch fire, a muffled cry rose up, people rescued the inhabitants and dragged them out, the fire-hoses sputtered and fizzed. "Do you enjoy that?" asked the pilgrim. "Well, when I make a direct hit, sure. Of course those guys put up things that act as protection, today I only made a bull's-eye on a couple o' bulls, not far from the house. Now I gotta slide this cloud down somewheres else." "What," asked the pilgrim, holding his ears, "what must people down there think of this?" "All kinds of things," the old man wheeled around and held off thundering, "that's the best fun of all! What does a fly think of the swatter? I tell you, there ain't nothin' like it! You should read some of this testimony! You know, once I single-handedly thundered this scientist guy in his lab, he had a lightning rod. The jerk grabbed like crazy at all his indicator dials, took readings, made notes. I laughed myself silly and thundered so rapid-fire the boob could hardly keep up. He was a weird one!'' The old man laughed till he cried and sent down more thunder. Then he bade the pilgrim farewell, shook hands with him and rode off on his cloud to another district.

THE ARTISTIC CABARET NEVER FORMALLY DEVELOPED IN ITALY, but the avant-garde movements there were nourished by a thriving popular variety stage. One of the greatest stars of Italian vaudeville, hook-nosed, falsetto-voiced Ettore Petrolini (1886-1921) began his career in 1903 at a seedy café-chantant that had a 30-cent entrance fee. He honed his skills in the smoke-filled variety theatres of the Piazza Guglielmo Peppe, and by 1912 was famous throughout Italy. He went into revue in 1915, but never found it congenial to his talent, for he excelled as a purveyor of pure nonsense in the short *macchietta* or solo character sketch interrupted by improvisations. He revelled in the *slittamento* or side-step, breaking character to comment on a theatrical mishap, put down a heckler or, Pirandello-like, strip bare the actor-audience relationship. There was an abrasive, skeptical, disrespectful, destructive aspect to his comedy that greatly resembles the adversarial spirit of the early cabaret.

Petrolini was lauded by the intelligentsia, described as a modern comedian *dell'arte*, the Great God Pan, the grotesque in action. Marinetti (see below) praised "his pure futuristic humor" and his robot-like mask Fortunello whose "mechanical and monotonous rhythm, its pounding toof-toof to the infinite absurd and grotesque rhymes, bored spiralling tunnels of stupor and illogical, inexplicable merriment into the audience." Petrolini was himself to write a one-act play with the Futurist Cangiullo.

The Driver's Handbook
(Manuale dello chauffeur)
1915
by
Ettore Petrolini

Special training you don't need
To drive a car at any speed:
If you will this handbook read,
I wrote it for that purpose . . .

All right! Since I love cars more than anything else on earth, I wanted to compile a handbook for the perfect driver. Read it, and you'll find everything you need. My compendium can serve ladies as well as gentlemen: . . . it's that big! . . . I'll offer some proof of it, because it gives me pleasure when each of you sees it and touches it with your hand.

That's most important!

When you ask the dealer for 30 horse-power, make sure he doesn't give you a squadron of cavalry. And be careful that the horses don't have charley horses or hoarse throats. And keep as far away as you can from the fillies: they get too expensive!. . . Next, I advise you to acquire a thirty-first horse, of flesh and blood, to help pull the other thirty when they get tired . . .

That's most important! . . .

When it comes to wheels, always pick a well-known brand. I believe the best wheel is the one for the lottery . . .

That's most important!

The inflatable tire is composed of an air chamber and the tire proper. The tire proper is inseparable from the air chamber: if you don't have the tire proper, you don't need the chamber; if you're missing the chamber, the tire proper's no good . . .

A little chamber is sufficient: there are good ones from three francs up by the hour . . . The driver is always expected to pay for the chamber.

That's most important! . . .

The tire proper often has a red circle painted on it. A lot of people complain because, after few kilometers, the red wears off. But just the opposite happens to me: the more I use the car, the deeper I get in the red! . . .

That's most important! . . .

When the rubber springs a leak, seal it right away! If you're travelling with a lady, make a point of keeping an eye on the rubber. As soon as you find an opening, block it up immediately, if only with your finger . . .

That's most important! . . .

If you're on a honeymoon trip, take the generator out of your car and replace it with a good regenerator . . .

That's most important! . . .

The gas tank is filled from a can. When the can is empty, it is more than likely that the tank is full. With my wife, this rarely happens!

That's most important! . . .

Lubrication . . . Some people lubricate with oil, some people lubricate with kerosene . . . I've always found it best to lubricate with vaseline . . .

That's most important! . . .

The exhaust pipe . . . The exhaust pipe can be kept closed or opened, as you please . . . Women had better not keep theirs open, to avoid loose talk . . .

That's most important! . . .

Of the major openings on the automobile, some are furnished with a metal lining, known more exactly as a bush. These are most important and most delicate. You're in trouble if they break! . . . Insist that they be made of pure bronze and manufactured with the greatest care . . . For greater security, I always handle the bush myself . . .

That's most important! . . .

The pump, which is used to blow up the rubber tire, must be

durable and easy to manipulate. Pump with precaution, fill'er up every so often and stroke the rubber to determine the degree of hardness . . .

That's most important! . . .

Starting up. Let'er out slowly, increase speed gradually, until you're in fourth gear . . . Don't overdo things: you may skid and run off the road. That's happened to me and I can assure you that it's a tiresome business getting back on the track . . . Generally I go 65 kilometers an hour; sometimes, to satisfy my wife, I get up to 66 or 67 . . . Just once I made it to 68; but I've never made 69 . . . It's too dangerous: you run the risk of losing all your benzoline . . .

That's most important! . . .

It is never advisable to try and take a back road as a detour . . . You've got to have lots of practice for that. It's a specialty of a certain German make! . . .

That's most important! . . .

In conclusion, some good advice to the gentlemen: if you have a blowout going uphill or your motor breaks down: get out at once and work it by hand! . . .

That's most important! . . .

OF ALL THE AVANT-GARDE ARTISTIC MOVEMENTS OF THE EARLY twentieth-century, Futurism was the one most reliant on performance. The term was coined by the Italian writer Filippo Tomasso Marinetti (1876-1944), only after discarding Electricism and Dynamicism. It burst forth on the world in 1909 with cries of "Burn the Museums!" when a preliminary manifesto was published in *Le Figaro*, asserting a Nietzschean will to power. From 1910, Marinetti and his colleagues sought direct confrontation with the public, and developed the notion of "bruitism" or dynamic sound.

An expanded "Manifesto del Teatro futuristico sintetica" published in Milan in 1915 called for a new form of drama, "the short acted-out poem, the dramatized sensation." The Futurists looked to the music hall and the variety theatre as models of vitality and interaction between performer and spectators. The rapid succession of disparate attractions, the carefree, unselfconscious atmosphere, the "dynamism" (a Futurist touchstone) were to be copied. They wanted to "compress into a few minutes, into a few words and gestures, innumerable situations, sensibilities, ideas, sensations, facts, and symbols . . . Our acts can be moments only a few seconds long."

The result was the *sintesi* or syntheses which compress "the diversity of life itself, a diversity present for a *moment* in a tram, in a café, at a station, and which remained filmed on our minds as dynamic, fragmentary symphonies of gestures, words, noises, and lights." There was no need to explain the meaning of these syntheses, nor had they to follow ordinary logic. One of the functions of the synthesis was to embody a new ideal of male/female relationships, since it is "a school for sincerity for man because it exalts his rapacious instinct and snatches every veil from woman. All the phrases, all the sighs, all the romantic sobs that mask and deform her."

Simultaneity may be Marinetti's best known synthesis, an interpenetration of two ways of life; the tart's impinging on the regulated and unwitting bourgeois family is like an oblique echo of

Ibsen's *Ghosts*. *The Toy Theatre of Love* is a more symbolist work, in which every aspect of environment including the furniture is imbued with life and contributes to the atmosphere. *The Communicating Vessels* manages to digest an epic series of actions and a lifetime into a few moments' stage time.

In September 1921 Marinetti and Francesco Cangiullo founded the Theatre of Surprise at the Hôtel de Londres, Naples, and the Company of the Theatre of Surprise debuted at the Teatro Mercadante the next month. These syntheses were meant to be a direct assault on audience expectations. The orchestra was dispersed throughout the hall: a trombone in a box, a contrabass in the stalls, a violin in the pit, the bass drum in the upper balcony, all conducted by Cangiullo who leaned out of a box waving a walking-stick for a baton. The walking-stick also came in handy as personal defense, for these ''demonstrations'' were often followed by fist-fights, police raids, and even the arrival of fire engines.

Naturally, a Theatre of Surprise manifesto ensued with a description of actual performances, three of which are given below. The first to be played, with Mussolini in the audience, was ''Music for Dressing By,'' which Marinetti wrote with Gianni Calderone. It is noteworthy that one of the best performers in the Theatre of Surprise was Ettore Petrolini.

Simultaneity. Interpenetration

(Simultaneita. Compenetrazione)

1915

by

Filippo Marinetti

A room. The wall right is entirely covered by a large bookcase. A little to the left a big table. Along the wall left, modest, lower-middle-class furniture and a door. In the wall at back a window revealing a snow-covered landscape, and a door opening onto stairs.

Around the table, beneath a shaded hanging lamp, whose light is dim and greenish, sits a middle-class family: The Mother is sewing, The Father is reading the paper, The Sixteen-year-old Son is doing homework, The Fifteen-year-old Daughter is sewing.

In front of the bookcase, but some slight distance from it, the most sumptuous, most magnificent dressing table, with mirror and candelabra, covered with all sorts of little bottles, flacons, and utensils used by a lady of the utmost elegance. A most intense beam of electric light envelopes this dressing table, at which is seated a young Tart, very beautiful, blonde, in a luxurious low-cut peignoir. She has finished doing her hair, and is intent on giving the final touches to her face, arms, hands, attentively assisted by an immaculate lady's maid, who stands aside but alert. The family does not see this scene.

THE MOTHER: (*To the Father.*) Do you want to go over the household accounts?

THE FATHER: I'll look at them later.

(*He returns to his reading. Silence. Everyone, in a natural way, goes on with what he was doing. The Tart, on her side, continues adorning herself, invisible to the family. The lady's maid, as if she has heard the doorbell ring, goes to the door upstage, opens it and lets in a messenger-boy, who comes over to the Tart and presents her with a bouquet of flowers and a note. The Tart smells the flowers, places them on the dressing table, reads the note. The messenger-boy exits with a respectful bow. The Sixteen-year-old lad rises shortly thereafter, goes to the bookcase, passing very close to the dressing table, as if it weren't there, takes a book, recrosses the room, comes back and sits at the table and starts to read.*)

THE SIXTEEN-YEAR-OLD: (*Breaking off his reading and looking out the window.*) It's still snowing . . . How quiet it is!

THE FATHER: This house is really too isolated. Next year we'll move . . .

(*The Tart's maid goes back to the upstage door, as if she has heard the bell ring again, and shows in a milliner's girl who comes over to the Tart and takes from her box a magnificent hat. The Tart tries it on at the mirror, gets annoyed because she doesn't like it and puts it aside. Then she tips the girl and dismisses her with a gesture. The girl exits with a curtsey. Suddenly the Mother, who has searched the table, gets up and goes out the door left, as if to fetch something she is missing. The Father gets up, goes to the window and stands looking out the panes. Little by little, the children fall asleep at the table. The Tart leaves the dressing table, slowly and cautiously approaches the table, takes the account-book, the homework, the sewing, and nonchalantly throws it all under the table.*)

THE TART: Sleep!

(*And she slowly returns to the dressing table, and starts to clean her nails.*)

CURTAIN

Note

In *Simultaneity* I have put on stage the simultaneous interpretation of the life of a middle-class family with that of a Tart. The Tart is not a symbol, but a synthesis of sensations of luxury, disorder, adventure, dissipation, which dwell, with anguish, desire, or regret, in the nervous system of all the persons seated around the peaceful family table.

Simultaneity is an absolute autonomous theatrical synthesis, since it is assimilated neither in the middle-class family nor in the life of the Tart, but in itself. Simultaneity is as well an absolutely dynamic theatrical synthesis. As a matter of fact, whereas in a drama like [D'Annunzio's] More than Love, the important facts (e.g., the murder of the owner of the gambling casino) do not take place on stage but get told with an absolute lack of dynamism; whereas in Act One of [D'Annunzio's] Jorio's Daughter, the facts do take place on stage, but with too external and, if one may say so, cinematic a realism, in my synthesis Simultaneity I achieve an absolute dynamism of time and space, with the simultaneous interpenetration of two different ambiences and several different times.

The Toy Theatre of Love
Drama of Objects
(Il Teatrino dell'amore. Dramma d'oggetti)

Dining room. Upstage, two doors, one of which opens into a library. On the left wall, two doors, between them the Buffet. On the right wall, a door, the window, the Sideboard. Center, a Table with chairs. Moderate lighting.

THE LITTLE GIRL: Mama, let me stay with you a little while longer . . . In your bed. May I?
THE WIFE: No, no. It's midnight. You should be asleep. You know I don't want to see you with circles under your eyes . . . You're tired . . . Go to bed . . . Come on, that'sss right. Go on.

(The Little Girl exits slowly through one of the doors left. The Wife waits until the sound of her footsteps fades out in the back of the house, then exits through the door right that leads to her room, putting out the light. Silence. The furniture creaks testing its strength sotto voce.)

THE BUFFET: Creak. It'll rain for three quarters of an hour. (*Silence.*) Greeeeel. Someone's opening the front door. (*Silence.*) Creak. Creak. The pressure of the silverware is beyond my cohesion!

THE SIDEBOARD: Crack crack. On the fourth floor the servant is going to bed. (*Silence.*) On the stairs is a weight of 70 kg. (*Silence.*) Crack.

(*The Husband, wearing a dressing-gown, enters through the other door left, with a small shaded lamp, crosses the room, goes to the library seen upstage. Hesitating before the shelves, he picks out a large book, then slowly recrosses the room, carrying the heavy book. The book slips from his hand. It thuds on to the floor. Silence. He picks up the book, then exits through the same door he entered by. The Wife enters through the right door, stands listening, goes on tiptoe and opens the door to the stairs. The First Comer enters, an elegant young man, carrying a voluminous bag.* Quiet! Sssh! . . . *Quiet! The First Comer opens the bag and pulls out a little toy theatre, which he places on the table.*)

THE WIFE: (*In an undertone.*) Lovely! Lovely! (*With childlike delight and wonder, clapping her hands noiselessly.*) Thank you . . . Come . . . (*She leads him towards the door right. They leave. The door closes again. Silence.*)

THE BUFFET: Creak. It's raining . . . it's raining . . .

THE SIDEBOARD: Crack. The master's back is sticking little by little to the back of the armchair.

(*The Little Girl in a nightgown enters through the first door left, gropes her way to the table in the dim light, stands listening, then goes toward the door right—the Mother's room—and stands there eavesdropping.*)

THE SIDEBOARD: Craack.

(*The Little Girl hears a step approaching from her Mother's room, and runs to crouch under the table. The door right opens.*)

THE WIFE: (*Stepping into the doorway, stands a moment listening.*) Nothing . . . They're all asleep. (*Withdraws, shutting the door.*)

(The Little Girl emerges from under the table, stands a long while listening, then nods her head, lays it on her arm curled up on the carpet and goes to sleep. From the moment when the toy theatre was put down, an actor hidden behind the table has set the marionettes in motion.)

THE BUFFET: Creak. It's raining.
THE SIDEBOARD: Craack. I'm splitting.

(Silence. The door right opens again. The Wife enters, in a state of undress, followed by the First Comer. They do not see the Little Girl under the table. The Wife goes to the sideboard, opens it, takes out a liqueur bottle and two glasses, which she puts on the table. She drinks. They kiss. The First Comer exits through the door to the stairs. The Wife spots the Little Girl, wakes her up and shows her the toy theatre.)

THE LITTLE GIRL: *(Rubbing her eyes.)* Lovely! lovely! *(Utters these words with the same intonation of childish delight and wonder with which the Wife first uttered them. Brief silence.)* I was dreaming. *(Takes the toy theatre and lets herself be led back to the first door left.)*
THE SIDEBOARD: Craack. Craack!

CURTAIN

Note

In *Toy Theatre of Love*, I wanted to present the life not of humans but of objects. The most important characters are the little wooden theatre (whose marionettes perform in the dark without the presence of a puppeteer), the Buffet, the Sideboard (which are not on the traditional stage), but they present in a non-human way the temperature, their dilations, the weight that they support, the vibrations of the walls, etc.

These three characters live in the nerves of the nervous Little Girl, while she listens at her Mother's door. The wooden toy theatre is the symbol of futility, fugacity, and theatricality of romantic attraction, and its marionettes act in the dark, inexplicably, just like the amorous movements of the two characters who are embracing in the next room. There should result a significant parallelism between the illogical delight the Mother manifests at the sight of the plaything, and the real delight the Little Girl experiences when the Mother offers it to her, leading her to bed.

The Communicating Vessels

(I Vasi comunicanti)

The stage is divided into three parts, by means of two partitions. —Section 1 (left): Mortuary Chapel. Bier center, surrounded by large lighted candles, priests praying, numerous relations of the deceased. —Section 2 (center): A street; in front of the door of an inn a table and a bench on which a woman is seated. —Section 3 (right): A rural landscape, trenches not far from the forestage. As the curtain rises, in Section 1, the priests mutter prayers and the relations wail: "oooooooooooooo."—Suddenly a voice from the relations: "A pickpocket!" And the pickpocket is seen forcing his way through and running down to the forestage; he walks around the first partition, enters Section 2, and sits down next to the lady, with whom he drinks and talks.—Meanwhile, on the street, a lot of soldiers head towards the forestage.

A SOLDIER: (*To the Thief.*) Come with us!
THE THIEF: Sure I'll come! To die for my country! (*Gets up.*)
THE LADY: (*Holding him back.*) What! Now that we're in love and happy, you're leaving me? (*Weeps.*)

(*The Thief wards off the Lady and blends in with the soldiers, who, going round the second partition, enter Section 3 and occupy the trenches.*)

AN OFFICER: Pow! Pow! (*Fires, then:*) Forward! Break down that wall! Forward!

(*The soldiers leave the trenches, run upstage, break down the second partition, crowd into Section 2 again, and move across it.*)

THE OFFICER: (*In front of the first partition.*) Break down this wall too, to outflank the enemy!

(*The soldiers break down the first partition too, invade Section 1 and move across it tumultuously, knocking over the bier and the candles, dispersing the relations. When they reach the wings left, they suddenly fall back, struck dead in a row.*)

CURTAIN

The Theatre of Surprise
(Il Teatro della Sopresa)
1921
by
Filippo Marinetti, Gianni Calderone, and Francesco Cangiullo

A Simultaneity of Voluptuous War
A Theatrical Surprise

The poet Marinetti declaims his *Battle of the Fog*, excerpted from his romance *The Steel Alcove*, accompanied by an invisible kettledrum which imitates bombardment. Two elegant dancers, a man (in a swallow-tail coat) and a woman (dressed in a low-necked pink outfit) dance an extremely languid tango during the declamation.

Penetration of the combattants' state of mind, a mixture of bellicose fury and nostalgic sensuality. This tango-interspersed recitation was also performed by the voices of Marinetti and the Futurist poet Guglielmo Jannelli.

Note

This Futurist invention has invariably—even on the most riotous evenings—the prodigious power of riveting the emotional admiration of the entire audience, which, after listening attentively, bursts into a stormy ovation.

Music for Dressing By
A Theatrical Surprise

An upright black piano has its legs shod in two elegant gilded ballerina's slippers. An actor, the piano's maid, dusts the keyboard, tinkling over it absent-mindedly with a feather-duster. At the same time, a second actor (the second maid) gently rubs the teeth of the piano with a little brush, while a hotel bellboy in red livery runs a woolen pocket-handkerchief over the gilded pedals of the piano.

CURTAIN

Note

This surprise provoked another surprise on the other side of the proscenium. A gentleman, turning to Marinetti who was watching from a box, cried: "You aren't crazy, but you're driving everyone else crazy." At the same instant, at the parapet of the gallery, an individual began to whistle violently, then suddenly burst into applause. The gentleman in the pit then cried: "There's the first case of insanity," and made off in terror.

Public Gardens
A Theatrical Surprise

To the left of the spectators:
Two Lovers (actor and actress) are hugging and kissing on a park-bench.

To the right of the spectators:
A big picture from *The Surprise Alphabet*, showing three wet-nurses portrayed by three enormous W's; each one with a suckling at her breast in the form of an 8.
  A typical invert behaves effeminately.

Downstage:
6 automobile riders (*five actors and one actress*) seated without support, like the other 4, simulate the bouncing and swaying of 5 persons in an automobile, with the relevant driver who imitates all

the noises.

CURTAIN

Note

At Lucca, just when the curtain came down, a spectator, walking on his hands with his legs in the air, did a flip from the gallery stairs.

At Turin, a spectator, disguised as Cavour, harangued the public, in contradistinction to another spectator, disguised as Mazzini.

ZURICH, DURING THE WAR, WAS A HAVEN FOR PACIFISTS AND anti-establishment types from all over Europe. There the senseless annihilation going on outside Switzerland could be observed with a certain degree of detachment, and the DADA movement meant to mirror this debacle of Western civilization by demolishing art and even language.

The literary forum for this movement, even before it got its name, opened on 5 February 1916 at the Meierei Hotel as the Cabaret Voltaire. Its founders were Hugo Ball (1886-1927), a German poet and director who had studied directing in Berlin before the war, and his future wife, the singer Emmy Hennings. Ball's declared intention was ''to remind the world that there are persons of independent minds—beyond war and nationalism—who live for different ideals.'' Participants at opening night were the Rumanian painter Marcel Janco, the Rumanian poet Tristan Tzara (Sami Rosenstock, 1896-1961), and the Alsatian poet and artist Hans (Jean) Arp. The first program included recitations of poems by Blaise Cendrars, Max Jacob, Vasili Kandinsky, Else Lasker-Schüller, and Christian Morgenstern, among others, along with piano music by Debussy, Scriabin, and Schoenberg.

The truly provocative aspect of the cabaret was added by the German physician Richard Huelsenbeck (1898-1974), as he recited poetry with polemically broken syntax to a heavily rhythmic drum beat. With Tzara as conductor, Huelsenbeck and Janco would recite simultaneously in German, English, and French, accompanied by the ''bruitistic'' noises of rattles, pipes, and howls. This so-called ''simultaneous poetry'' was supposed to show the human voice, a manifestation of the soul, irretrievably adrift in the mechanical indifference of the modern world. ''Cultural and artistic ideals as the program of a variety theatre, that's our way of reacting like Candide against the era,'' proclaimed Ball.

The Cabaret Voltaire began to put out a newspaper with the same name, and in 1917 a ''DADA Gallery'' was opened with ''abstract'' dance, new music and puppetry; it usurped the cabaret's function and was available to a wider public. As a result, the purity of the artistic experiment became tainted by a desire to *épater* the world at large. It was an arena for many avant-garde movements for exponents of Futurism (Marinetti), proto-expressionism (Kandinsky), and proto-surrealism (Apollinaire) presented their words and images there, and Emmy Hennings sang Hugo Ball's ''Dance of Death.''

Dialogue Between a Coachman and a Lark

(Dialogue entre un Cocher et une Alouette)

1916

by

Richard Huelsenbeck and Tristan Tzara

HUELSENBECK (COACHMAN): Hüho, hüho. Ich grüsse dich, o Lerche. (*Heigh-ho, heigh-ho. I greet thee, o Lark.*)

TZARA (LARK): Bonjour, M. Huelsenbeck.

HUELSENBECK (COACHMAN): Was sagt mir dein Gesang von der Zeitschrift Dada? (*What has thy song to say to me about the Dada newspaper?*)

TZARA (LARK): Aha aha aha aha aha (*fortissimo*) aha aha (*decrescendo*) cri cri.

HUELSENBECK (COACHMAN): Eine Kuh? Ein Pferd? Eine Strassenreinigungmaschine? Ein Piano? (*A cow? A horse? A street-cleaning machine? A piano?*)

TZARA (LARK): Le hérisson céleste s'est effrondré dans la terre qui cracha sa boue intérieure je tourne auréole des continents je tourne je tourne consolateur. (*The celestial hedgehog sank into the earth which spat out its inner mud I turn aureole of continents I turn I turn comforter.*)

HUELSENBECK (COACHMAN): Der Himmel springt im Baumwollfetzen auf. Die Bäume gehen mit geschwollenen Bäuchen um. (*The sky leaps up in cotton rags. The trees walk about with swollen bellies.*)

TZARA (LARK): Parce que le premier numéro de la Revue Dada paraît le 1 août 1916. Prix: 1 fr. Rédaction et administration: Spiegelgasse 1, Zürich; elle n'a aucune relation avec la guerre et tente une activité moderne internationale hi hi hi hi. (*Because the first issue of the Dada Revue comes out on August 1st, 1916. Price: 1 franc. Editorial offices: Spiegel Street 1, Zurich; it has nothing to do with the war and is attempting an international modern activity hee hee hee hee.*)

HUELSENBECK (COACHMAN): O ja, ich sah—Dada kam aus dem Leib eines Pferdes als Blumenkorb. Dada platzte als Eiterbeule aus dem Schornstein eines Wolkenkratzers, o ja, ich sah Dada—als Embryo der violetten Krokodile flog Zinnoberschwanz. (*Oh yes, I saw—Dada came out of a horse's body as a flower-basket. Dada burst like an abscess out of the chimney of a skyscraper, oh yes, I saw Dada—as the embryo of the violet crocodile flew a cinnabar tail.*)

TZARA (LARK): Ça sent mauvais et je m'en vais dans le bleu sonore antipyrine j'entends l'appel liquide des hippopotames. (*It smells bad and I am going off into the sonorous antipyretic blue I hear the liquid call of hippopotami.*)

HUELSENBECK (COACHMAN): Olululu Olululu Dada ist gross Dada ist schön. Olululu pette pette pette pette pette . . . (*Olululu Olululu Dada is great Dada is beautiful. Olululu fartta fartta fartta fartta fartta . . .*)

TZARA (LARK): Pourquoi est-ce que vous pettez avec tant d'enthousiasme? (*Why do you fart with such enthusiasm?*)

HUELSENBECK (COACHMAN): (*Pulling a book by the poet Däubler out of his pocket.*) pfffft pette pfffft pette pfffft pette pfffft pette . . .
O Tzara o!
O Embryo!
O Haupt voll Blut und Wunden.
Dein Bauchhaar brüllt—
Dein Steissbein quillt—
Und ist mit Stroh umwunden . . .
Oo Ok du bist doch sonst nicht so!
(*O Tzara o!*
O Embryo!
O Head full of blood and wounds.
Your belly-hair bellows—
Your coccyx gushes—
And is wound round with straw . . .
Oo Ok otherwise you would not be that way!)

TZARA (LARK):
O Huelsenbeck, O Huelsenbeck
Quelle fleur tenez-vous dans le bec?
C'est votre talent qu'on dit excellent
Actuellement caca d'alouette
Quelle fleur tenez-vous dans le bec?
Et vous faites toujours: pette
Comme un poète allemand.
(*O Huelsenbeck, O Huelsenbeck*
What flower do you hold in your beak?
Is it your talent, said to be excellent
Currently lark's doodoo
What flower do you hold in your beak?
And you keep going: fartta
Like a German poet.)

AS A DISTINCT ART MOVEMENT, DADA HAD DIFFICULTY AFTER
the war maintaining its autonomy. Tzara moved to Paris, where he
was rapidly overwhelmed by the burgeoning Surrealist movement.
Hugo Ball broke away from DADA in 1917, feeling that its alleged
poetry of revolt was a demonstration of diabolical egotism, neither
poetic nor creative: "the safety valve of an abstract age has burst."
Berlin, reeling from the overthrow of the Kaiser and spasms of
political anarchy, proved temporarily congenial to a reconstituted
DADA with a more political program: art as a weapon of class war-
fare. Huelsenbeck, the poet and essayist Walter Mehring (see
Cabaret Performance: Europe 1920-1940), and the painter Raoul
Hausmann (1886-1971) founded a DADA-Club, which held its
first meeting on 12 April 1918, reviving Huelsenbeck's "Phantas-
tical Prayers" and "Bruitistic Litanies" from the Cabaret Voltaire.

Hausmann, an anarchist, had earlier been connected with a
radical leftist expressionist group of artists in Dresden, and he
deplored DADA's previous disinterest in politics. Using violent,
strident photomontages, he tried to promote a program of social and
political idealism. The most unrestrained of the Berlin DADAists
was the architect Johannes Baader, the self-announced "Ober-
dada," given to statements like "Dada is the cabaret of the world as
much as the world is the Cabaret Dada. Dada is God, spirit, matter,
and roast veal." Faced with such enthusiasm, Huelsenbeck went off
on a trip round the world as a ship's doctor in 1918.

Then, for a time, the DADA impulse found a haven in another
literary cabaret. Max Reinhardt had taken over the Schumann Circus to house his Grosses Schauspielhaus; in the former stables in the
basement he set up a second Schall und Rauch. The opening night,
8 December 1919, promised to be similar to the first: the composer Friedrich Hollaender was in charge of music, the actors included the excellent cabaret artistes Blandine Ebinger and Paul
Graetz, and the *pièce de résistance* was a parody of the *Oresteia*
being given upstairs on the main stage, here performed by life-sized
puppets made from designs by George Grosz. But the premiere end-

ed in a riot provoked by the Dadaists, who shouted ''Long live art! Down with Reinhardt!'' This was answered by the countercry, ''Down with the Dadaists!''

Reinhardt was unoffended, and the cabaret, whose managers fancied themselves avant-garde, for a time housed literary and artistic experimentation for the post-war generation. Mehring set his macaronic lyrics to ragtime rhythms; Joachim Ringelnatz was introduced to a Berlin public. Another discovery was Klabund (Alfred Henschke, 1890-1928), whose pseudonym came half from *Klabautermann* (bogey man) and half from *Vagabund* (tramp). As a student in Munich, he had come under the influence of Wedekind and Morgenstern, and his sardonic, slangy ballads had earned him too an obscenity trial. A pacifist, Klabund appeared in Zurich at the Cabaret Voltaire in 1917, but even in Switzerland his outspokenness won him a brief jail sentence. Back in Berlin, he became a leading purveyor for the Schall und Rauch of anti-bourgeois songs, which, Tucholsky said, ''whistle, howl, scream, and squawk'' to music. His cryptic, alienated ''grotesques'' proved to be more philosophical and elegaic than most cabaret material.

The problem was the cabaret's size; with 1100 seats, it had to appeal to a more general audience. Before Arp, Schwitters, Tzara, and others formally interred DADA at the Weimar Bauhausfest in 1922, the second Schall und Rauch managed briefly to be a seedbed for cabaret satire. But, as Kurt Tucholsky regretted, ''a proper literary cabaret just wouldn't go. It's a great big shame.'' When Reinhardt gave up the Grosses Schauspielhaus, the Schall und Rauch dwindled into a mere entertainment cabaret and ended up as a beer joint in 1924.

Of the material given here, Hausmann's sketch ''Genius in a Jiffy'' or ''Instant Genius'') parodies the attitudes of the general public to the Dadaistic influence at the Schall und Rauch. ''Engineer Dada'' is John Heartfield, who cast the Oresteia puppets in plaster; the ''Dadasophist'' is Hausmann himself. (Mehring was known as the ''Pipi-Dada.'') Klabund's ''The Gambler'' is a typical ''grotesque.''

Genius in a Jiffy or a Dadalogy

(Der Geist im Handumdrehen oder eine Dadalogie)

1920
by
Raoul Hausmann

The stage is horribly dark, breakfast rolls rain down in the moonlight. A house once stood left. Out of the past enters Engineer Dada followed by the Dadasophist.

ENGINEER DADA: I feel so abandoned.—My eyes indeed were the first to see the light, but in the present revolutionary atmosphere . . . I believe something is bound to happen. The same thing goes for Byronic collars and penny-dreadful poetry. Otherwise things'll get very bad. I'd like to sing a song. A little bit of art. (*He sings.*)

> Herr Hölz he plays the gramophone,
> It drives Herr Ebert mad,
> Herr Seeckt's behind the fence alone,
> And wants to bash him bad.

A good song, a beautiful song. And yet people say I have bad teeth. Those nitwits, the Dadaists; when I think of the meatheads there are who understand nothing about taking photographs. For example there's the Dadasophist, imagines he could be something. Nothing but a . . . hush, here he comes now.

DADASOPHIST: Ah, good morning, Engineer, I'm glad I ran into you. Button up my left ear for me, I have until this evening to write a poem for ''Schall und Rauch,'' but I've sprained my hand and can't reach my head.

ENGINEER DADA: You are a nasty fellow. You ask me to do things you wouldn't do yourself. I'll have Grosz make a sketch of you, so you can see just how ugly you are. But strain your brain for 5.75 marks, no soldier in the Baltic provinces makes that much, it's overpaying—and concoct a political poem. You can't do it by yourself, I must first engineer it properly. You Prague stevedore!

DADASOPHIST: I—I need just a piece of paper—and then my chamberpot brain whizzes away like a spinning top.—Give me a kick, you capitalist wage-slave, it'll do my stomach good and then you'll see.

ENGINEER DADA: (*Boxes his ears.*)

DADASOPHIST: (*Blubbers.*)

> The fat bourgeois guzzles a bottle of wine,
> At night screws his dear wife in bed,
> Hopes his hero Herr Kapp will manage just fine,—
> And then the dumb ARPshole drops dead!!

—there! didn't I say so? good, right?

ENGINEER DADA: Why, man—You're bigger than Mehring and Huelsenbeck put together. Kerr will have to deliver a revised verdict on you and I myself will raise your honorarium to six marks. You must see to it that Kurt Wolff publishes you, perhaps under the title: My name is Rolf or I am a Beast; man, you ought to give me ten marks for that! That's an invaluable idea! Straight from me!

DADASOPHIST: Man, I may have a trust-fund, but I have to pay so much luxury tax I cannot give you any money. I would rather recite another poem. Listen:

> Let malicious people rap,
> Profiteering's there for all.
> Goods? nah, just hand out pure crap,
> Profiteering leads the ball.
> Sure, laws against it have been framed,
> But if your granddad's clever,
> If Sklarz or Scheidemann he's named,
> No laws can hurt you ever!
> So, man, it's clear for all to see
> You're totally secure!
> Go profiteering stalwartly,
> In good company, be sure:

Ebert, Fritze, the Kaiser, it appears,
Are all enrolled among the profiteers.

ENGINEER DADA: Oh, that won't do—nope, nope, NOPE—it won't work if you dare list our illustrious sovereign as a profiteer! Suppress that! When I was back in New York at the Nocker Bocker, a fellow dared make indecent remarks about President Wilson—well, I can tell you, it made me feel very bad—believe you me. I had to leave America right away and that affected the exchange rate so adversely for me that I wished there had been another big Kapp or rather Ludendorff uprising, because if I were to film it, the rate of exchange would go up again. But now—well, bore a hole in the asphalt, take a telescope and then you can keep an eye on the exchange rate! Otherwise, if nothing special happens, they'll say I've engineered the world atlas of the Dadaists, the Dadaco, so well that Hänisch will order a million copies for school textbooks! By the way, my man, dadaism—well, what exactly is it?

(Both break into a lament, the sky turns light blue, blood and walking-sticks rain down,—both Dadaists are eaten up by two Berlin Daily editors, and a voice from the audience says:)

Dada's a hoax!
Is there an anti-Semite organizer in the house?

Translator's Notes

The name-dropping refers to the turbulent political and artistic scene in post-war Germany. Max Hölz, a Spartacist, in 1920 had led a Communist revolt in Vogtland which he proclaimed a Soviet Republic; he was a promoter of the General Strike of 1921. Wolfgang Kapp had led a monarchist revolt against the republican government, seized Berlin and had himself proclaimed imperial chancellor; he was abetted by half-mad General Erich Ludendorff, who was later a participant in the Hitler beer-hall Putsch. The revolt failed after the general strike, and Friedrich Ebert resumed power as first president of the German Reich. Hans von Seekt, a military hero, was commander-in-chief of the Reichswehr; Phillip Scheidemann, who had urged a compromise peace during the war, was proclaimed first Prime Minister of the republic but resigned when the Reichstag accepted the terms of the Treaty of Versailles.

Konrad Hänisch, a Social Democrat and Minister for Public Worship and Education, had convened a Schoolbook Conference in 1920.

For Hans Arp, Richard Huelsenbeck, Walter Mehring, and George Grosz, see above. Alfred Kerr was Berlin's most influential drama critic. Kurt Wolff founded a new publishing house devoted to avant-garde and experimental works.

The Gambler

(Der Spieler)

A Scene

1920

by

Klabund

The gambler is staggering across the stage in a green tail-coat, a green top-hat, and an orange cape.

I've lost . . . I've lost it all . . . I'm finished . . . before I had even begun . . . I had four queens in my hand . . . Four queens all at once . . . ha, I thought, at last Fortune is smiling to the fourth power . . . I bet ten thousand . . . my opponent was a skeleton dressed in the latest fashion . . . a monstrous pumpkin-sized skull . . . no hair, no flesh . . . No eyes, the five cards of a poker-hand held motionless in his bony fingers . . . The skeleton squeaked out twenty-thousand like a badly oiled velocipede. The man, I thought, if he actually is a man, is crazy, totally idiotic . . . I've got four queens in my hand, and he wants to up the ante, I shout 40,000 and my head rang, throbbed with this verse:

> When Lady Luck comes as a fourfold treat,
> A man roams the fields, a fog in his head.
> What cares he for women in home or in street
> Or the narcissus wind when the twilight turns red?

80,000 cackled the skeleton . . . That's called making the best of one's cards to the very last . . . You are life and he is death . . . You have the world to win from him . . . Ah, immeasurable luck, if you win eternal bliss . . . immortality. 160,000 I roared . . . 320,000 echoed the rattling anatomy . . . I computed feverishly . . . 160 and 80 and 40 and 20 and 10 . . . total 310 thousand . . . all my faculties were in play and at stake . . . What could I bet against his 320,000? Behind my chair stood Evelina . . . fair and delicate and sweet as ever . . . she had gone pale . . . I turned around . . . I lifted my arm onto the gaming-table . . . She closed her eyes and stood still as a statuette . . . then I tore the silken dress from her body . . . and her shift . . . She stood naked on the table . . . And I cry: Against your 320,000 I bet my wife and my girl, my beloved and my goddess . . . Agreed? The skeleton grinned and ran his empty eye-holes over the blooming flesh of the young female body . . . Agreed, it bleated its assent, Evelina stood there leaning to one side . . . We tossed our cards on the table . . . he had four aces . . . I saw him wrap his black cape around Evelina . . . and lift her from the table . . . I heard his tinny voice order a car from a club waiter . . . I stumbled out into the black night . . . My fate is sealed . . . soon the apple trees will bloom again . . . I shall learn English at the Berlitz school, I have a talent for languages and I'll write for American newspapers and magazines . . . which pay fabulously, really fabulously . . . 1000 dollars an article with illustrations . . . now . . . I should get hold of a camera and take pictures of everything . . . simply everything . . . 1000 dollars makes, hold on a minute, at the current rate of exchange 20,000 marks. 20 articles and I'll have won Evelina back . . . ah, it's not as bad as it looks . . . Gambling, that's the only way to train for life and fate . . . Even as an embryo I was in the habit of playing baccarat . . . as you'd expect, I won . . . I won in this way in a single stroke a thousand marks, which I put aside, to defray the costs of my year as a military volunteer later on . . . for my parents were simple people, my father sold supplies for delicatessens, my mother was working on her degree in philology . . . Kindred interests brought them together, a holy sympathy of the heart . . . It was a love-match, the kind you see in novels. My mother made me suckle the breasts of knowledge, which she exerted significantly less than if they were her own . . .

My father's educational method was limited to providing or withholding smoked herrings, carob beans, American canned goods. So practical knowhow and ideology maintained an equilibrium in my education . . . At the age of five a comet fell on my head, giving it a somewhat squashed and flattened shape . . . At the same time it was taken as a sign from heaven that I was marked out for great things

. . . When I was nine, nine . . . is the number of baccarat, mark that well, Edward the Seventh of England lost India to me in a game of baccarat . . . I became Viceroy of India, which position I fully sustained until my thirteenth year . . . Then I handed the crown back into the hands of his English majesty . . . It was, incidentally, only thinly gilded . . . Since that day I could never stop gambling . . . But I kept losing, even my mind, which I had to pay a hundred marks for; for to have luck . . . you must have money . . . and to have money . . . you must have luck . . . Luck determines what a man has . . . Luck is what lots of money can buy: an afternoon at a jazz tea at the Paradise Bar . . . Price, a hundred marks . . . Supper with Fern Andra . . . just to be seen with her . . . at Hiller's or someplace like that . . . Price, 1000 marks . . . a visit to Madame X in Z Street, where you can meet a few flappers . . . Price, 2000 marks . . . And finally two hours at a gambling club, alias the Union of Young Friends of Terrariums . . . Price, . . . ty marks . . . Lend me 50 marks . . . I'll bet it all on one card . . . if I win, I'll buy a zebra or a spring cloud . . . Lovely money . . . people find nicknames for money they might otherwise apply to a woman . . . Who would believe from my patent-leather shoes and the crease in my trousers that I have no money, an elegant beggar . . . that's the worst thing . . . I'll go to a first-class hotel and live a few weeks on credit, I can't get any in a second-class hotel . . . it's a miserable life . . . Should I go on as an eccentric dancer at the Korso Theatre? Ah, lovely gold and lovely cards, and lovely, lovely women . . . Queen of Diamonds . . . and Queen of Spades . . . and Queen of Clubs . . . and Queen of Hearts.

Oh, I'll go to Korso Theatre . . . and dance . . .

(*Eccentric Dance*)

ONE OF THE ARTISTS WHOM HUELSENBECK REFUSED TO ADMIT to the Berlin DADA-Club was Kurt Schwitters (1887-1948), considering him too apathetic to politics. Schwitters was opposed to Huelsenbeck's aesthetic program which asserted, "All in all, art should get a good thrashing." In 1920, he wrote that there were two kinds of Dadaists, the "kernel" kind and the "husk" (in German, *Huels*) kind, and insisted that the entire environment contains the ingredients of art. Schwitters experimented with collages of disjunct found objects, which he called MERZ, and extended this to a poetry patched together from overheard conversations, lines from pop songs and the like. The muse of Schwitter's poetry, which he recited at his own cabaret evenings in Hanover, was Anna Blume. His collections of verse *Anna Blume* and *Die Blume Anna* (*Blume* meaning flower) appeared in 1919 and 1924; they were comparatively traditional syntactically, but Schwitters used them to explore verbal iconography. He also conceived of a MERZ Theatre that would detonate all the possibilities of the stage.

Schwitters described the musical portion of a MERZ performance in this way: "Now the passion of musical impregnation begins. Backstage organs sing and say 'Fitt Fitt.' The sewing machine clatters forward. A man in one of the wings says 'Bah.' Another suddenly comes on and says: 'I am stupid.' (Copyright reserved.) A minister on the other hand kneels in between and shouts and prays aloud: 'O grace abounding to be wondered at. Hallelujah youth, youth weds drops of water.' A water-main drips monotonously unhampered. Eight. Drums and flutes flash death, and a streetcar-conductor's whistle shines brightly. A stream of ice-cold water runs down the back of the man in one of the wings into a pot. While he sings C sharp D, D sharp E flat, the whole workers' song. A gas flame has been lit under the pot to boil the water, and a violin melody shimmers pure and maiden-like. A scarf overbroadens breadths. The midst of the passion boils deep dark-red. It rustles slightly. Long sighs from the violin surge into crescendo and fade away. Light darkens the stage, and the sewing machine goes dark too."

To Anna Blume
(An Anna Blume)
by
Kurt Schwitters

O you, beloved of my twenty-seven senses, I
Love you!—You your yourself yours, I, you, me.
—We?
Which (incidentally) is no way concerned with this.
Who are you, untold female creature? You are
—are you?—People say you might be,—let
Them talk, they do not know how the church tower stands.
You wear your hat on your feet and wander on
Your hands, on your hands do you wander.
Hello, your red dress, sewn into white pleats.
Red I love, Anna Blume, red I love you!—You your
Yourself yours, I you, you me.—We?
Which (incidentally) is concerned with cold embers.
Red bloom, red Anna Blume, what do people say?
Prize question: 1. Anna Blume has a bird.
    2. Anna Blume is red.
    3. What color is the bird?
Blue is the color of your yellow hair.
Red is the cooing of your green bird.
You modest girl in everyday clothes, you dear green beast,
I love you!—You your yourself yours, I you, you me,
—We?
Which (incidentally) is concerned with the ash-bin.
Anna Blume! Anna, a-n-n-a, I drip your name.
Your name drips like soft beef suet.

Do you know it, Anna, you do really know it?
You can be read backwards, and you, you
Most marvelous of all, you are behind as you are before:
"a-n-n-a."
Beef suet trickles in streaks down my back.
Anna Blume, you dripping beast, I love you!

A Futurist evening. Sketch by Umberto Boccioni, 1911.

A "freewordist" design by Francesco Cangiullo (1917), later used for the Theatre of Surprise piece Public Garden *(1921). Since the Italian word wetnurse is* balia, *the figures are shaped like B's, not W's as in the translation given here.*

*A poster by Kurt Schwitters for a Merz-matinée,
featuring an Anna Blume poem.*

*This typographical
layout of* Dialogue
Between a Coachman
and a Lark *was com-
posed by Marcel
Janco for the journal*
Cabaret Voltaire,
1916. *It contains por-
traits of Huelsenbeck,
left, and Tzara, right.*

Richard Huelsenbeck
and Raoul Hausmann
in civilian clothes.

Ettore Petrolini in his one-man
sketch The Little Sausages, 1911.

Walter Mehring as the
Pipi-Dada. A collage
from the Schall und
Rauch magazine,
May 1920.